THE STEP BY STEP ART OF
STENCILLING

THE STEP BY STEP ART OF
STENCILLING

GILLIE SPARGO

JG
PRESS

4108
Published in the USA 1996 by JG Press
Distributed by World Publications, Inc.
Copyright © 1995 by CLB Publishing
Godalming, Surrey, UK
All rights reserved
No part of this book may be reproduced or
transmitted in any form or by any means, electronic
or mechanical, including photocopying, recording,
or by any information storage and retrieval system,
without permission in writing from the Publisher.
Printed and bound in Singapore
ISBN 1-57215-188-9

The JG Press imprint is a trademark of JG Press, Inc.
455 Somerset Avenue
North Dighton, MA 02764

CONTENTS

MATERIALS & EQUIPMENT

Preparing for stencilling

Before you can start the process of stencilling you must have something to stencil on! This book will show you how to prepare a variety of items using materials readily available from do-it-yourself or art stores.

Old furniture is best stripped and then painted or left with a natural wood surface. Strip off any old finish with **paint** or **varnish remover**, wearing **protective gloves.** Otherwise, engage a professional stripper, who will use either acid or a non-caustic stripper.

Sand your wood or metal smooth with **wire wool** or **sand paper**, both available in three basic grades. Fill holes and cracks with **fine surface filler** for wood or **car body filler** for metal.

Repair wood with **quick-drying glue**. **PVA** (polyvinyl acetate) **medium** is a versatile, non-toxic glue that can be used for sticking paper and fabric.

Invest in a couple of good quality **paint** and **artist's brushes**. Use **white spirit** to clean your brushes after using oil-based paints like gloss and eggshell.

For a few of the projects you may need some more unusual sounding items such as **acrylic gesso** (from art stores) to make grainy wood seem smooth, **a steel rule** or a **heartgrainer** to simulate the grain lines of wood.

Occasionally, a **jigsaw** is needed to cut holes in the centre of a wooden sheet, but if you prefer you can ask a local carpenter to do this for you.

In addition, it is a good idea to save **newspapers**, **glass jars** with lids, **plastic containers** and **old rags**, all of which you will need for these projects.

Cutting a stencil

Stencilling is achieved by applying paint through holes cut in either **oiled Manilla card** or **plastic film**. Craft suppliers and good art stores stock card in sizes 38 x 51 cm (15 x 20 in) and 51 x 76 cm (20 x 30 in). It is ready for use, having been 'oiled' in manufacture. Plastic film comes in numerous shapes and sizes, generally on the small side, in clear, blue and opaque white varieties. It has the great advantage of being see-through, but is costly and harder to cut than the card.

To mark your design on card, use a sharp **2B pencil** or **permanent marker pen**. To copy a template from the back of the book, use **tracing paper** and **typist's carbon** (available from stationers). Very large sheets of **dressmaker's carbon** made can be bought at haberdashers.

To cut a stencil in either card or film, use a sharp **craft knife,** but nothing too heavy or with a bulky handle. The scalpel shown in this book has **removable blades**, sold in packets of five in stationers and art stores.

Stencilling

Keeping your stencil firmly in place while you are applying the colour is essential. Use **spray adhesive** (from art stores), which, although tacky enough to adhere the stencil to any clean, dry surface, enables you to peel the stencil off without leaving any residual glue, and to reposition it again and again before respraying. For an intricate stencil it is really unbeatable, but **masking tape** stuck all around the outer edge of the card or film will suffice as long as care is taken not to lift up any delicate parts of the stencil while working.

Liquid stencil paints are available in small quantities (but go a long, long, way) and in a wide range of colours. There are two kinds. **Hard-surface paints** are exactly that, for use on firm surfaces such as walls and furniture, while **fabric paints** are for textiles. **Oil-based crayons** come in a limited range of colours. They need cleaning from time to time with **white spirit**.

Stencil brush sizes start at 5 mm (³⁄₁₆ in) and go up to several centimetres (approximately 1½ in) across. Try to have a separate brush for each colour. Wash them clean with **cellulose thinners** (available from car accessory stores) as soon as you have finished using them to extend their useful life.

Finishing

Your object for stencilling does not have to have a plain, painted colour as a base. Make it more interesting by trying some of the simple paint techniques suggested in the projects to add interest and texture underneath your motifs. 'Dragging' with a specialist **dragging brush** – or a **wallpaper brush** – produces a series of soft lines. Sponging (use a **natural sponge** only) gives a more textured effect. Try your hand at reproducing the effect of liming, but only on areas not to be stencilled, or colour wood in unusual shades before you start your stencilling.

After all your hard work in preparation and stencilling, protect your work with a coat of **varnish** if possible. On furniture, use a polyurethane **varnish** in a choice of matt, satin or gloss. Protect tiles with special **ceramic varnish**. An interesting kind of varnish available from art stores, **crackle glaze**, will give your model an 'antique' effect. Different manufacturers produce crackle glazes that vary in technique so read the instructions carefully before starting. In general, it is a two-part varnish, which when left to dry leaves small or large cracks on the surface that can be coloured with thinned artist's oil paint to produce the antique effect.

Cleaning

Do not attempt to clean an area of stencilling with anything stronger than a **damp cloth** and a little **dish-washing liquid**. Do not rub or soak your newly painted model or you will damage the paint (though sometimes worn paint can look old and interesting).

If stencilling on glass with stencil paints, it will be necessary to paint on a coat of protective varnish to enable thorough cleaning. When cleaning glass, test an inconspicuous area first with a stick wrapped in cotton wool. Do not use window cleaning fluids.

TECHNIQUES

THE SAME BASIC techniques occur in many of the projects used in this book. Before starting any project, it is important that you take the time to read through the techniques needed and to practise the methods used.

Prepare your surface thoroughly before beginning stencilling. Follow the cutting techniques carefully to ensure that your stencils last for a long time and start by using the recommended stencilling technique for each project. With time and more experience you will be able to make you own decisions about paints and techniques. Finally, do not worry if you make a mistake by smudging the stencil as this can be remedied using the right materials.

Stripping wood

Preparation is all important to a good finish. Remove old paint or varnish, stripping by hand with a stripping agent (always protect your hands with rubber gloves), or send to a professional stripper. On flat surfaces, use a metal scraper to remove the worst of the surface. On curves and to reach into crevices, apply stripper on a brush and remove using wire wool.

Preparing wood

After stripping, the object will need sanding to achieve a smooth surface on which to apply your chosen finish. Use various grades of glasspaper or wire wool, coarse first, then medium, then finish with fine. Before painting, brush down with a dry paintbrush and wipe with a clean rag dampened in white spirit. This lifts off any dust and dries quickly.

Applying paint

Paints are divided between water- or oil-based types. Water-based paints are emulsions and acrylics, which dry quickly and can be cleaned with water. Oil-based paints are gloss and eggshell. They dry much more slowly and need to be cleaned with white spirit. Self-undercoating and eggshell varieties can be painted straight onto prepared wood.

Detailing by hand

The two stencils used for this cat's head, body and feature markings would, stencilled alone, result in a rather crude image. By adding details, a very realistic picture can be achieved. Here, a photograph has been used for reference. The head and body have been coloured to resemble the photograph, with the features and markings in appropriate colours. An artist's brush has then been used to outline and highlight the eyes and to add whiskers and hairs.

Marbling

  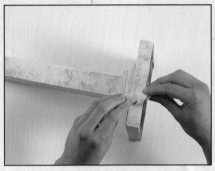 

1 Remove any finish or varnish and sand smooth with glasspaper or wire wool (see opposite). Paint with two coats of white eggshell. Allow to dry. Mix two glazes (see page 15). Dampen a natural sponge with white spirit, squeeze out any excess and dip into one glaze. Dab randomly all over the surface. Clean the sponge with white spirit and warm, soapy water. Repeat with the second glaze. When marbling, do not stop between steps, not even to make a coffee, you must not let the glazes dry out!

2 To soften the dappling effect of sponging, lightly flick all over with the softening brush to blend the two shades of glaze. (Alternatively, use a good quality paintbrush with thick, tightly-packed bristles.) Soak a clean rag in white spirit and use to wipe any excess paint from the bristles of the softening brush. Do this several times while you work.

3 Soak a small piece of clean rag in white spirit and wring out any excess. Roll the rag up, making sure there are creases in it. Gently roll it over the entire surface, slightly changing direction all the time. Wash it out in more white spirit to clean, or use a new piece once it becomes covered in paint. This technique lifts the glaze off in varying degrees.

4 Mix three glazes for painting in the veining. Mix the darkest one from artist's oil paints (viridian and raw umber) and white spirit only. Mix two further shades of glaze adding cadmium yellow to veridian in two different strengths. Use a separate artist's brush for each glaze, one thin, one larger and one square-ended, to add variation and width to the veins. Paint veins in all over. Twist the brush as you work to vary the line and overlap the two colours.

5 Brush over the veining with the softening brush, using a light flicking movement. Flick in one direction only as this is how veining occurs naturally. The 'softening' should merge all the colours and blend the veins into the background in some places and not in others. Leave to dry. If you do not like the effect, wipe off with white spirit and start again.

Verdigris

1 Place the article on several layers of newspaper in a well-ventilated area and spray with a can of copper-coloured paint. Repeat several times for an even finish. In a glass jar, pour a little dark emerald green matt emulsion paint. Dilute 2:1 with water. Paint over the copper – it will not cover evenly – and allow to dry.

2 Using a separate brush for each colour, dab on the three verdigris pastes (see opposite) at random over the article. Do not quite cover the emerald green emulsion. Store any remaining paste with a lid on. The paste will keep for a few weeks. Thin if necessary with methylated spirits.

3 Do not stop for a break between the stages of applying the pastes. The verdigris needs to be kept damp. Carefully spoon some of the whiting into a cooking seive and gently rub it through the mesh with the underside of the spoon so that it coats the wet verdigris pastes.

4 With a household paintbrush, flick over the entire surface of the frame to remove any excess whiting. Using the same brush dipped in clean water, wash over the whole frame to slightly dampen it. This will 'set' the whiting and blend it with the pastes.

5 Continue working without breaking off so the whiting does not dry. Gently rub over the complete frame with medium or fine grade wire wool. The aim is to leave patches of the pastes intact, to allow the emerald emulsion to show through and also to rub through to the copper layer. The ingredients used in this method of verdigris will not withstand being left outdoors.

Mixing glazes

Glazes are thin washes of coloured paint, generally pale shades, applied over a base coat that then still shows through. Ready-made glazes are available from specialist paint firms.

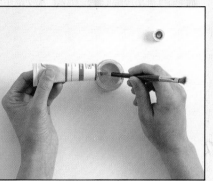

1 Pour a little white eggshell paint into a glass jar and add artist's oil colour (or any coloured oil-based paint) bit by bit, mixing together thoroughly with a brush before adding more colour. If the colour seems too deep, add more white eggshell or preferably another artist's oil paint to lighten and create an individual shade.

Verdigris paste

1 Take three glass bowls and place four or five spoonfuls of whiting into each (whiting is a dry, plaster-like substance, available from specialist decorating stores). Buy small sample pots of matt emulsion paint in two shades of minty green and one shade of pale blue.

2 Add some blue emulsion to one of the bowls and mix thoroughly with an artist's paintbrush to form a dry paste. Thin with methylated spirits until the paste becomes the consistency of thick double cream. Repeat in the two remaining bowls with the two shades of green emulsion, using a separate brush for each colour.

2 Thin the glaze with white spirit, adding a little at a time and mixing it in thoroughly, until you have the consistency of thin cream. Store with the lid firmly closed. Should you leave the glaze for some time before using, it may thicken slightly. Add white spirit to thin. Darker tones of glaze can be made, thinning oil-based paint or artist's oils with white spirit only (do not add white eggshell). These have a tendency to dry out and ought to be used immediately.

Making and cutting stencils

Stencils for the projects in this book should be cut from oiled Manilla card unless otherwise specified.

Adapting a drawing

1 Trace templates directly onto plastic film using a fine marker pen. For Manilla card, trace the template onto tracing paper. Trace over these outlines onto stencil card, inserting typing carbon in between. Where two or more stencils are needed to complete an image, trace and cut the main outline from one piece of card, then cut any details onto one or more pieces of card. The body and head of this cat were cut on one stencil, its eyes, nose and markings on another.

2 Cut around the outlines of the design. To cut any stencil, no matter how simple, you will require a sharp craft knife and a cutting board (self-healing plastic is excellent) or a sheet of glass (though this will blunt blades very quickly). This stencil is made up of two seemingly unrelated elements, a bold cross and delicate flowers whose bridges are narrow in keeping with the intricacy of the design.

3 The two stencils which make up the teddy design are very much related. One stencil has all the body pieces, separated by narrow 'bridges'. The other has all the details that give the teddy its character. To help in tracing off the correct parts of each stencil onto the separate card pieces, shade in all the details for the second stencil. This one will obviously be stencilled last after the main part of the motif.

The sketch of the rag doll reading her book, drawn from a real doll and not a template, requires a small adaptation before it can be used as a tracing. To add a little realism to the figure, extra head and shoulders need putting back under her hair. This area is marked for clarity with red shading.

16

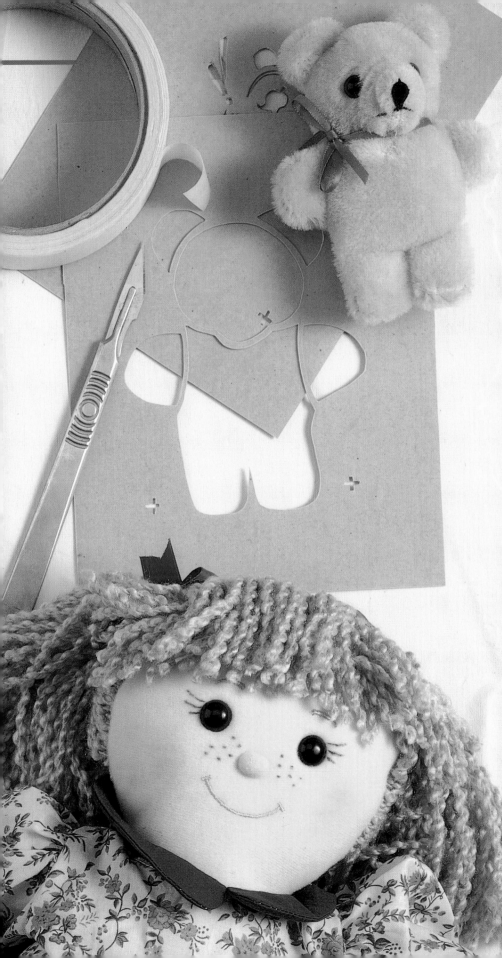

Repairing a stencil

Both stencil card and plastic film are relatively strong, but they can be damaged. In general it is the bridges that snap at one end. Stick broken ends back in place with small pieces of masking tape. Turn over and cut away any excess tape showing. Other vulnerable areas are parts joined at one end only. Re-attach with tape or cut a new piece and stick with tape.

2 Cut all the elements of the stencil. Position carefully over one another and fix together with masking tape on the free side where no form of registration mark is to be made. Place on a cutting board and trim off square. In this case the doll's 'back' edge was cut close to her body through all layers. Use a steel rule rather than a plastic ruler if you have one.

Registration marks

1 When two or more stencils make up a design, they will require some method of placing one exactly over another. This is done by cutting registration marks through all layers, usually in the form of a cross. When positioning the first element for stencilling, mark the crosses lightly with pencil. Position the second element with its crosses over the marks. Rub off the marks on completion of the project.

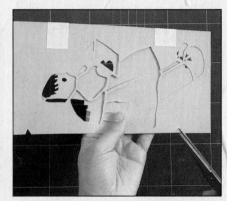

3 In certain situations, marking registration crosses is not the best method. In the case of the doll reading her book and leaning up against the door of the dresser there is limited room for crosses. It is better to cut out notches from her back edge for registration vertically, and to butt the stencil card up to the lower beading for horizontal registration.

Methods of stencilling

The various methods of applying paint all give a different finished result and it is this which determines the method you use. Each method has its advantages and disadvantages, but the brush method is probably the most versatile.

The brush method

1 Use a separate stencil brush for each colour. Decant a little hard-surface paint onto a washable dish. Dip the brush into the colour and dab off the excess onto kitchen paper towel.

2 Apply the paint through the stencil with a dabbing motion, starting at the centre. Dab on other colours to give the effect of shading or use a swirling movement without lifting the brush. The mixure of dabbing and swirling gives a lovely finish on completion. Get to know your brushes as each gives a different texture. This technique adds 'life' to the stencil. It is quick to dry and brushes wash clean in water. It can take time to work and large areas will take longer to cover than if using sponging.

A happy cross between the smoothness of crayons and the marked texture of sponging, stencilling by the brush method is the technique most commonly used.

The sponge method

1 Pour a little of each hard-surface paint required onto a washable dish. Break a natural sponge up into pieces for small areas of stencilling (the holes in man-made sponges are too even in texture). Use a separate, water-dampened sponge for each colour. Dab the sponge with paint and blot off the excess onto kitchen paper towel before applying.

2 The unevenness of the holes in the sponge give a definite texture. If the paint is applyed heavily, this starts to disappear. Sponging is quick to cover large areas and the sponges will wash clean in water for re-use. Natural sponge can be expensive, however, and you need to gauge carefully how much paint to blot off first.

The crayon method

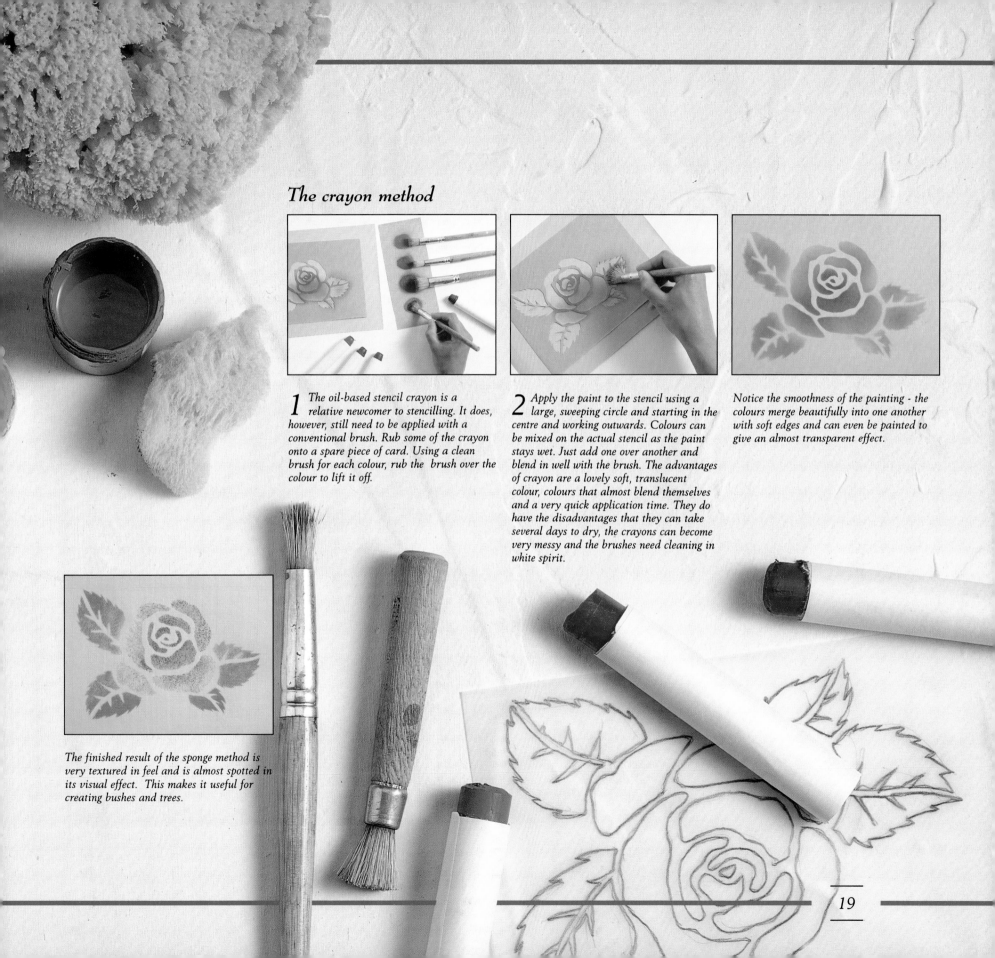

1 The oil-based stencil crayon is a relative newcomer to stencilling. It does, however, still need to be applied with a conventional brush. Rub some of the crayon onto a spare piece of card. Using a clean brush for each colour, rub the brush over the colour to lift it off.

2 Apply the paint to the stencil using a large, sweeping circle and starting in the centre and working outwards. Colours can be mixed on the actual stencil as the paint stays wet. Just add one over another and blend in well with the brush. The advantages of crayon are a lovely soft, translucent colour, colours that almost blend themselves and a very quick application time. They do have the disadvantages that they can take several days to dry, the crayons can become very messy and the brushes need cleaning in white spirit.

Notice the smoothness of the painting - the colours merge beautifully into one another with soft edges and can even be painted to give an almost transparent effect.

The finished result of the sponge method is very textured in feel and is almost spotted in its visual effect. This makes it useful for creating bushes and trees.

Cleaning up:
water-based paint

Masking tape, though wonderful for
providing a straight line to paint against,
always lets a little paint seep under the edge.
As soon as the paint is dry, remove the tape,
pulling it off cautiously. Using clean water
in a container and a clean rag, gently rub
off the unwanted paint. Keep changing to a
clean area of dampened rag.

Cleaning up:
oil-based paint

Here, the oil-based glaze has run
slightly onto the door edges during sponging.
Allow the glaze to dry before handling.
Remove the paint with cotton wool-wrapped
sticks dipped in white spirit, replacing the
stick when dirty. If applying a 'line' of glaze,
remove masking tape when the glaze is touch
dry, cleaning up any excess before the drying
process is finished.

Making piping

1 Piping cord is available in many widths. Choose one that is appropriate in scale or for the look that you require. Always wash piping cord before use as it shrinks considerably more than the fabric encasing it. A lot of hard work can be ruined otherwise on the first washing. Press fabric to remove any creases. Fold in half diagonally across the grain, that is, at an angle to the selvedges and the weave. This produces lengths of fabric that mould around corners easily. Mark the fold by pressing firmly along it with your fingernail to give a crease.

2 Open out the fabric. With a sharp pencil and ruler, lightly mark lines running parallel to the crease line about 4 cm (1½ in) apart. Using sharp fabric scissors, cut down the crease line made with the fingernail and along the pencil lines to make long strips of fabric for your piping.

3 Place two strips together with right sides facing and raw diagonal ends matching. It should look as though two points are sticking out, one to either side. Pin together and continue to piece the remaining strips together until you have a length long enough for your piping.

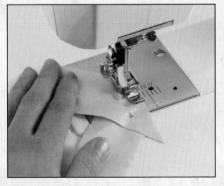

4 Thread up the sewing machine to match the colour of your fabric. Using the piping foot attachment, machine across the ends taking a 1 cm (³/₈ in) seam allowance, and removing the pins as you work. Use the width of the foot attachment as a guide, keeping the inner (right) side running parallel to the *raw edge*.

5 Trim off the excess fabric close to the stitching lines and press seams open. Lay the piping cord lengthways down the centre of the fabric on the wrong side. Wrap the fabric around the piping and pin in place on the right side. Machine as close to the piping as you can down the entire length of fabric. (The piping foot can be positioned to be right or left-handed.)

6 Starting on the bottom edge, place the piping around the outside edge of cushion front, with raw edges matching. Pin in place along the stitching line. At corners, snip through two layers of piping fabric only up to the stitching line. Where the ends of the piping meet, overlap them neatly. Cut off excess. Machine all around over the previous stitching, taking care at the overlap.

FURNITURE

Preparing, painting
and stencilling furniture is one of the most
rewarding ways of spending a quiet weekend.
If you have ever spent time looking for, but never
finding, that individual design in quite the right colour
then look no further to begin creating your own
custom-made pieces.

ROSE CHEST OF DRAWERS

THIS CHEST OF drawers was in a very sorry state. The old, brown varnish was chipped and scratched and there were a couple of gaping holes on the top and down one side where a backpiece and towel rail had originally been. Luckily all the handles existed and matched as these are difficult and expensive to replace if missing. A carpenter turned a new towel rail, fitting it in the old holes, and plugged the holes on top with circular pieces. It was then ready for its facelift!

1 Remove the handles. On Victorian chests the handles are usually backed with a turned wooden screw. Simply unscrew the complete handle and screw as one. Rub the varnish off the whole chest, wrapping glasspaper around a sanding or worn-out abrasive block. Wear old clothes and a face mask to protect you from the dust.

BELOW: Notice the shading in the stencilling. It adds realism and depth to the flowers and leaves. Try to use three or four pinks in each rose and two greens, plus yellow, brown or white in the foliage.

2 Clean any old glue and dirt from the screw part of the handles. Sand off the varnish using a flexible abrasive block, which is easy to rub into the grooves. After sanding, wipe the handles and chest down with a clean rag, dampened in white spirit (see page 12). Paint in off-white eggshell. Stand the handles in bottles or similar to dry.

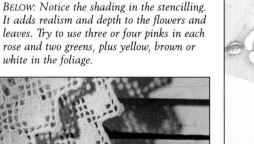

4 Trace and cut out the rose stencils on page 86 using plastic film (see page 16). Stencil the motif using the brush method (see page 18) and three shades of pink and green, two shades of blue, yellow and light brown, and white stencil paints. Use the whole stencil on one half of the lower, largest drawer if possible. To stencil one half of the next drawer, mask the stencil off until you have a design to fit the space available. Repeat for the outer edges of the top drawers. To stencil the other halves of the drawers, turn the stencil over. Clean, wetting kitchen paper towel with cellulose thinner and rubbing carefully over the dried paint. Fill in the middle of the drawers with the small rose and bow designs. Use the smaller elements of the design to decorate the top and frame of the chest, masking off unwanted areas as before.

3 The chest and handles will need two coats of off-white eggshell paint. Allow to dry thoroughly between coats and before decorating. Mix a small amount of dull pink glaze in a tiny glass jar (see page 15). Individual jam and marmalade pots are perfect for this purpose. Alternatively, choose a shade that you would like to be dominant in your design. Use a fine artist's brush to decorate the handles with delicate circles painted in the grooves.

5 To give the chest an instant antique look, wipe over with furniture wax. This is available in several tints, including 'antique'. Buffing may remove little bits of stencilling but adds to the aged look.

RIGHT: Having restored the chest to its former glory, try collecting a few pretty pieces to sit on it that are also antique, a swivel mirror, for instance, or a glass vase for flowers or some crochet-edged linen.

ORIENTAL WARDROBE

1 *Before stripping or sanding take an accurate reference of any details in case they become damaged. Take a rubbing with the flat side of a pencil onto tracing paper. Trace the rubbing onto stencil card and cut a stencil (see page 16). Note that it cannot always simply be cut out – here you would merely cut a circle with knobs – bridges must be added at each intersection .*

2 *To repair missing bits of moulded decoration, use the rubbing made for cutting the stencil. Trace the required area onto a piece of thin cardboard that is the same depth as the moulding (card from food packaging was suitable here). Carefully cut out the replacement piece, trying it for fit and trimming if necessary, and glue in place with all-purpose adhesive.*

NINETEEN-THIRTIES furniture is generally loved or loathed! Much of it is very heavy and cumbersome but some pieces, with a little imagination, can be made into something quite stunning and useful. This single wardrobe first appealed because of the chinese-looking raised decoration on the doors. That instantly suggested an oriental feel – one that was just as popular in the thirties as it still is today.

RIGHT: Painted and stencilled, a 1930s wardrobe becomes the focal point of the room. To decorate the room in keeping, try pasting oriental-style giftwrap inside wooden moulding on the walls and adding a few fans.

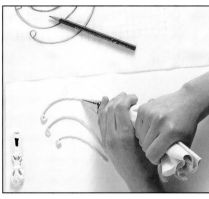

3 *Have large items stripped professionally as this is extremely time consuming by hand. Remove doors and hinges. Leave on any handles to be painted with gesso and with the background colour, making them merge in and disappear. Paint the entire wardrobe and doors with acrylic gesso until the grain of the wood no longer shows. Sand down with fine grade glass paper between coats. The gesso creates a smooth surface that is reminiscent of chinese lacquer.*

4 *Draw the bird and tree templates on page 87 onto tracing paper. Use the tracings to mark the position of the birds' tail feathers and the tree branches onto the wardrobe surface. Mix up interior plaster filler, spoon into a cake icing bag fitted with a small round nozzle and pipe carefully along the feather and branch lines. Allow to dry.*

ABOVE: This wardrobe had rounded moulding down the doors and edges, just waiting to be painted like bamboo! To copy this look, try gluing and pinning split bamboo cane in place before painting.

5 *Paint the wardrobe with approximately two coats of matt emulsion in Chinese red. Allow to dry. Pick out the branches of the tree with a little white paint. Use the tracings to cut stencils of the bird body and tree trunks (see page 16) and cut a Chinese circle stencil using the template on page 87 if there are no mouldings present on your wardrobe. Stencil the bird body, the tree trunks and the Chinese circle in gold and black stencil paints, using the brush method (see page 18). Stencil the circle onto the sides of the wardrobe as well as onto the front. To stencil the tree trunks, trim the stencil very close to the cut areas so that it fits in between the plaster branches.*

6 *A moulded beaded edge is often found on 1930s furniture. Copy this in 'stencil' spots. Use the flat end of a small stencil brush dipped in acrylic gold paint to dab dots along the bottom and top edges of the door and wardrobe frame. Pick out any beading, if you have it, in gold using finger-painting. Dip the end of your finger in acrylic gold paint and run gently over the surface to colour. Repeat on any original relief moulding.*

7 *Cut dragonfly stencils using the templates on page 87. Stencil in gold acrylic paint using the brush method and turning the stencil in different directions to create the impression of flying dragonflies. Paint any moulding to imitate bamboo, first painting bands and spots in gold then in black paint, marking in dots and notches. A feature of Chinese lacquer is its smooth, shiny finish. Paint with gloss varnish, checking that the gold paint will not be dulled by it.*

FLORAL CIRCULAR TABLE

1 Fastening catches can be attended to by an antique restorer or replaced at specialist hardware stores. Clean off dirt, any remaining finish and ink stains with a combination of methylated spirits and household bleach. Wearing household gloves, rub on methylated spirits with wire wool and attack any stains with bleach on cotton-covered sticks. Wipe off any residue with a clean rag and then with white spirit. Allow to dry. Repeat if necessary.

2 On the newly stripped wood mark six equal panels. Measure the table top at its widest point from side to side and from top to bottom, marking the centre point in each case. Place the straight edge of a protractor along one marking line with the 90° angle mark along the other. Mark in 60° and 120° angles. Repeat on the other half of the table. Draw in the complete lines from edge to edge, using a long rule.

3 Check the outer motif on page 88 will fit the panels on your table. Reduce or enlarge the template if necessary on a colour photocopier. You will need to cut three stencils for this motif. Trace off onto stencil card all the areas indicated with a black outline and cut out (see page 16). Repeat for the areas outlined with a dotted line for a second stencil, then trace off the remaining areas for the third stencil. Cut a separate stencil using the template on page 88 for the central motif.

THIS ANTIQUE tilt-top table had seen better days, or perhaps was just dearly loved and over-used. The wooden top was badly marked with ink stains – a legacy from writing love letters? One would like to think so. The fastening catch too was well worn and not too reliable at keeping the top in a horizontal position. All in all, it did not seem too wicked giving a Victorian antique piece of furniture a new lease of life with stencilling!

4 Use newspaper to mask off all but one panel. Position the masking tape directly over the drawn lines. In a clean glass jar, make up a glaze, mixing acrylic scumble glaze with a brown tint, both available from specialist paint stores. (Being acrylic, this glaze dries very quickly and the six panels can be treated in quick succession.) Paint onto the panel.

RIGHT: The table in its upright position takes up very little space The decoration is shown off here with the repeating design seen in full. Note how there are no 'bridges', the leaves and flowers all touch one another.

RIGHT: The marquetry stencil design was inspired by a Regency dining table. The original design would have been brightly coloured but it has now faded to lovely honey shades. It is these pale tones that were copied in the stencilling.

5 Immediately take up a heartgrainer. Holding the handle, gently rock the grainer across its curved surface while slowly pushing it away from you across the width of the panel, creating woodgraining as you go. Treat the whole panel. This wonderful tool is available in various sizes, to give grain lines from fine to bold. A medium one is used here.

6 When dry, remove the paper and mask off the next panel. Repeat the process until all panels are grained. Allow the final panel to dry. With a 3 mm ('/8 in) gap between, run two lengths of masking tape through the centre point and across the entire top on either side of the panel edges. Paint in cream acrylic to resemble ivory inlay. Dry and repeat twice, giving divisions between all panels. Finally stencil, registering the outer motif stencils as shown on page 17. Use the brush method (see page 18) and hard surface stencil paints in forest green, lemon, yellow, brown and fawn. Finish by stencilling the central motif.

TARTAN DINING CHAIRS

1 *There seemed to be two varnishes on these chairs. A heavy, thick sort on the flat backs and the fine version that can be effortlessly sanded off on the legs. Test parts of a piece of furniture with glasspaper first to see how easy it is to clean before trying paint stripper (see page 12). These chairs required several treatments of stripper to remove the finish.*

2 *Do not be put off buying chairs with rush seats that are covered with a grey fur. This mould is simply removed by wiping off with a dry cloth or a paper towel. Clean the entire seat with a cloth wrung out in water and detergent. Do not soak it and dry as quickly as possible. The spore causing the mould is in the air all year and lands when rush is wet.*

W HEN BOUGHT originally, there was only one of these chairs available, then amazingly a few weeks later an identical one was spotted. If possible, never split a pair of items – two not only look better, they are more valuable. The French bistro appearance of these chairs called for a simple but bold approach to the stencilling. A strongly patterned tartan that could be echoed in fabric and accessories seemed the most appropriate solution.

3 An economical way to colour wood after preparing it is with matt emulsion paint. Match the colour with that of the room's colour scheme, or choose an unusual shade like purple. This method works like purchased wood-stains, soaking quickly into the surface but showing the grain through. In a glass jar, dilute the emulsion 50:50 with water. Do not paint the whole chair at once.

4 Depending on the weather and humidity, leave for between a few seconds and ten minutes before wiping off excess paint with a clean cloth. On a hot summer's day or when it is bright and windy, only a few seconds can elapse before the paint is too dry to wipe away. Conversely, in cold, damp or very humid conditions, leave for up to ten minutes.

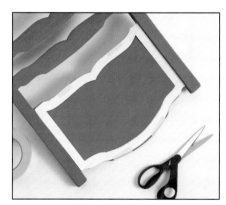

5 Cut a piece of tracing paper the width of the chair back from side to side. Lay the chair on its back, placing the tracing paper on the back-piece. With a pencil, mark the outline edge of the chair back onto the tracing. Cut out along the pencil marks. Place this template on thick paper and cut out. Mark a line 1.5 cm (⅝ in) in from the outer edge. Carefully cut away the centre.

LEFT: Take co-ordination to its limits – why not stencil the skirting boards to match the chair backs? Not the easiest of positions to stencil in – but the result is great fun!

6 Position the paper outline on the chair back with masking tape. Use the template on page 88 to cut three stencils (see page 16) on oblongs of card so the tartan design has straight edges. Position the stencils centrally over the chair to work. Using the brush method (see page 18) and hard surface stencil paints, stencil the lime green check first, then the lemon, then finally the red stripes. The template underneath creates a neat border outline.

HEART CUPBOARD

A LTHOUGH SMALL, this cupboard had many surfaces to adorn. It is made from solid oak and even before stripping off layers and layers of paint, the very textured grain of the oak was visible. Liming, an old treatment on wood, looks wonderful on the deep grain of oak and is brought up to date here with the addition of colour. The cut-out hearts in the back board became the inspiration for the stencilling.

1 Traditionally, liming was always white and was applied to woods like oak as a preservative to give a long-lasting wood an even greater life span. Liming wax can still be applied in white, though it is now fashionable to tint it. Place some of the wax in a glass bowl and add a teaspoon or two of powder colour in ultramarine. Mix well to the desired shade.

2 Paint the whole cupboard with a coat of matt emulsion in a slightly paler blue than the liming wax. The coloured wax will always be soft in colour because of the whiteness of the wax. When the emulsion is dry, rub the coloured wax onto the parts of the cupboard that are not to be stencilled. Apply it with fine wire wool, wearing rubber gloves if desired.

3 Rub the wax well into the grain of the wood. Leave for about five minutes to dry. Then, using a clean piece of rag, rub off any excess wax from the surface of the wood. The wax in the grain will remain there to emphasise the texture and give a hint of colour.

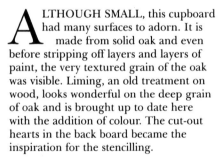

4 To set the wax in the grain and give a protective coating to the colour, rub the waxed areas with a neutral wax polish. Rub it in well with a clean cloth. This will remove a little of the colour but will buff up to a soft sheen, with another clean rag. Due to the waxy surface, it is not possible to stencil on limed areas.

5 Use the same soft blues and an apricot in emulsion paint to paint bands of colour along the flat edges of the cupboard. Employ a square-ended brush – its width determines the breadth of the band. When the decoration is dry, cut the stencils (see page 16), using the heart on a ribbon and heart grid templates on page 89. Stencil with

a brush (see page 18), using the illustration as a guide. Use green paint in addition to those mentioned above. The emulsion surface will wear with use, adding to the simple appeal of the cupboard.

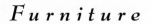

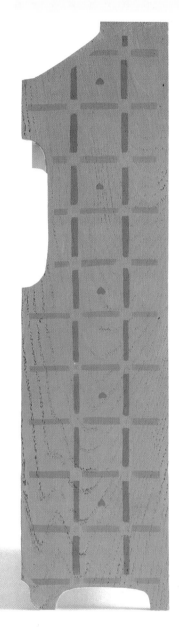

ABOVE: *The grain of the wood is visible here, even without liming. The cupboard is painted a soft shade of blue, taken from the Shaker palette and decorated with a simple stencil that imitates the Shaker style.*

LEFT: *Cupboards such as the one decorated here are a common find in antique fairs and flea markets. They make charming accessories for the house and provide useful storage space in kitchens and bathrooms.*

ART NOUVEAU FIREPLACE

I F YOU ARE fortunate enough to own a fireplace surround, it might be a little on the plain side and in need of decoration. Alternatively, it is possible to fit a new fireplace surround on an outside wall or into an existing chimney breast. Fireplaces do not have to be working to look good. Painting on a stencilled motif with the addition of an arrangement of dried flowers can create a stunning focal point in a room.

RIGHT: Follow the marbling instructions on page 13 to create a realistic marble effect for the mantelpiece. Use the honey glaze from the fire surround and make up a dark grey glaze from artist's oil paint and white spirit. Mix two beige/brown glazes for the sponging, referring to the instructions on page 15.

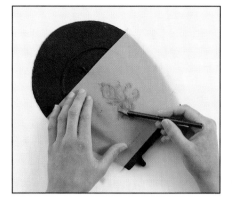

1 It is good design practice to take an existing decorative element present in one section of an object and to add it to another section in order to give some co-ordination. Here, a rubbing of the raised design on the hood flap was made with the flat side of a pencil onto tracing paper. The tracing was used to cut a stencil for the wooden surround. If you prefer, use the templates on page 89 to cut stencils (see page 16) of the art nouveau motifs that were used to decorate this plain surround, reducing or enlarging the motifs on a photocopier to fit.

2 This fireplace was bought for a song at an outdoor antique market because there was a crack in the hood, meaning it can never be used with a real fire. The thick rust was removed by professional sand-blasters, who immediately painted it with green oxide paint to prevent rust re-forming. The whole of the front metal surface was then painted with black iron paste, available from fireplace stores.

3 Rub the blacked grate vigorously with clean rags to create a soft, burnished look. Redo this periodically as the sheen will fade over time.

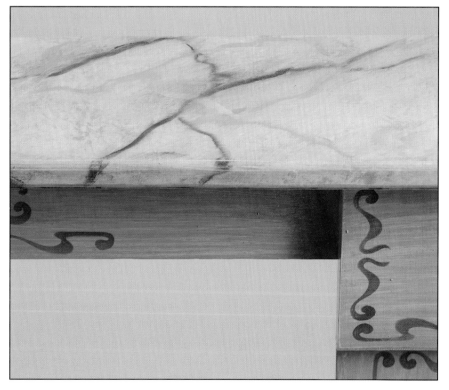

4 The wooden fireplace surround and mantlepiece were made by a local carpenter, who was instructed to make it very simple, with as many flat surfaces as possible as these are ideal to stencil. Surrounds can also be bought cheaply from household auctions and flea markets. Paint with several coats of cream eggshell (this also acts as an undercoat). When dry, mix up a honey-coloured glaze (see page 15) and paint on the flat surfaces.

5 *Using a very long-haired brush or a specially designed dragging brush, drag the wet glaze. Pull the brush through the glaze, keeping as much area of bristle flat on the glaze as possible. Wipe the excess glaze off the brush with a cloth dampened with white spirit. Do some of the dragging horizontally and some vertically. Clean up stray glaze from the edges of the surround with a cloth dampened in white spirit. Take care not to let the cloth catch on the dragged areas of painting.*

6 *Stencil, using several shades of green and red oil-based crayons for a soft look (see page 19). Use the colours separately or blended together to create new, differing shades. The surround will need to be left for several days to dry. Varnish if desired.*

LEFT: *Allow the stencilling to dry for two or three days before attempting to marble the mantlepiece or fix the surround in place. For non-working fireplaces, carpet can be laid right inside the fire for neatness.*

SEASIDE LINEN BASKET

WITH MORE AND more interest developing in conservation and doing things up, a great many old and odd bits of furniture are being brought out of retirement to give them a further life span. Objects made in this Lloyd Loom-type of weave are suddenly flooding the market. Some pieces are quite ordinary, but others like this linen basket catch the eye because of their wonderful 1930s shape and, of course, because of their practicality and usefulness.

RIGHT: The introduction of metallic paint for this project hints at the silvery sparkle sunlight makes on the sea and the flash of swimming fish. Emphasize the seaside and watery feel of the sponging on the basket with a flight of scallop shells glued to the wall 1930s style. A hot glue gun is invaluable here.

  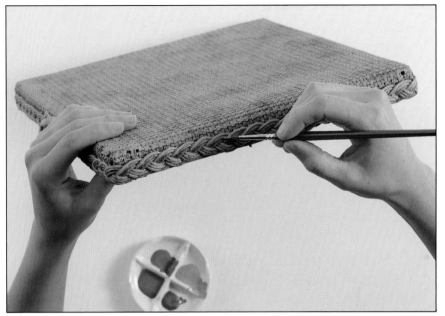

1 As the basket had been heavily re-painted in the past, it was sent to a professional stripper for cleaning up. Their process 'wets' the object less than doing it by hand and it is the damp that ruckles the weave. Remove the lid. Clean any rust and remaining paint off the handles with metal and chrome polish (available from car accessory stores), rubbed on with a clean cloth.

2 This weave has a disadvantage. Over years of repainting, the holes become clogged. Never paint this or Lloyd Loom by hand, always spray paint it with car spray paints or aerosol cans. The weave will be very absorbant for the first few coats. Make up a glaze from dark blue oil-based paint and white spirit (see page 15), sponging over randomly to create an underwater effect.

3 Make the most of a woven edge to the lid and basket sides by picking out the individual strands in bright blue, green and metallic red acrylic paints. This is quite painstaking but well worth the effort. Follow one strand all around in one colour, using a medium-sized artist's brush.

ABOVE: *The very textured finish of this woven surface softens the edges of the stencilling, making it merge into the background as though it were underwater.*

4 Because of the very textured surface, a stencil will not lie perfectly flat on it. It is therefore essential to use stencils with very little detail and with bold and strong shapes. Use the templates on page 90 to cut a sea urchin and two shell stencils (see page 16). Spray the back of the stencil with spray adhesive well, before positioning on the basket. Make a mask from paper to protect the surrounding area. Spray using metallic car paints in blue, green and red.

FABRIC

It is so easy to design and print your own fabrics with stencilling. Fabric paint is simple to use and may be washed with care. Decorate anything from a small cushion to entire curtains to give your home an ornate finish and delight your children by stencilling their favourite character or animal.

NOAH'S ARK COT QUILT

EVERYONE SEEMS to delight in making things for children. Perhaps it is just to see that look of enchantment on their faces, especially if the object depicts some of their best-loved characters or stories. This Noah's Ark quilt is bound to find a safe haven on a child's bed. Try making it into a wallhanging and a pile of cushions or stencil a border of marching animals around the room, ending at the ark.

ABOVE: To stencil the second squirrel in reverse, clean the used stencil with cellulose thinner and turn the stencil over.

ABOVE: The giraffe is positioned slightly off-centre in the fabric square. Notice the shading of the markings stencilled on it.

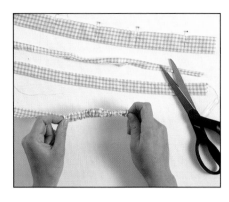

1 The tied bows at the bottom of the quilt are for decoration only. Cut six 40 x 6 cm (15½ x 2¼ in) pieces of check fabric in a contrasting colour to the quilt. Fold in half down their length and pin. Machine along one short end and down the length, taking a 1 cm (⅜ in) seam. Turn through to the right side and press well. Put to one side.

2 From plain cotton fabric, cut eight blue and seven white squares, all measuring 22 cm (8½ in) square. Cut stencils, using the templates on pages 90–91, from 20 cm (8 in) squares of card (see page 16). Tape the squares of fabric firmly to a flat surface – kitchen worktops are ideal. Using the illustration as a guide, stencil the animal motifs in appropriate colours – yellow, brown, beige and grey. Stencil the waves, the ark, Noah and his wife in shades of blue, adding red to the ark. Use the brush method (see page 16) and keep the stencils in place with spray adhesive. Note that the giraffe, and Noah and his wife templates are not centred on the square.

3 Lay the squares out in order with right sides up. Machine-sew into horizontal sets of three, taking 1 cm (⅜ in) turnings and with right sides facing. Now sew the five horizontal sets together along their top and bottom edges, taking the same seam allowance as before and with right sides facing. Press the seams open on the reverse side and set the paint according to the manufacturer's instructions.

4 For the border, cut two pieces of large-checked blue gingham 102 x 24 cm (40 x 9½ in) for the sides and two pieces 106 x 24 cm (42 x 9½ in) for the top and bottom. Machine sew the side borders in place taking 1 cm (⅜ in) seams and having right sides facing. Add the top and bottom pieces, right sides facing, joining them to the squares and the side borders and taking 1 cm (⅜ in) seams. Press all seams open.

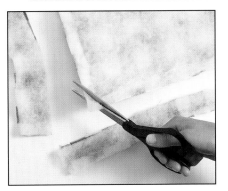

5 *From large-checked blue gingham fabric, cut a piece for the back measuring 106 x 146 cm (42 x 57½ in), joining lengths if necessary. Cut a similar sized piece from light-weight polyester wadding for the padding. Lay the back piece out with the right side up. Over it, place the front piece with the wrong side up and cover both with the wadding.*

6 *Pin the three layers (top, back and wadding) together around the top and side edges, taking a generous seam allowance of 3 cm (1⅛ in) and leaving a gap of 76 cm (30 in) at the bottom. Trim off the excess to 1 cm (⅜ in) and cut off all corners close to the stitching line. Turn the quilt right side out. Trim wadding along the open edge, turn in 3 cm (1⅛ in) to the inside at the front and back, tucking in the three pairs of ties at regular intervals. Sew the gap closed.*

7 *Lay the quilt out flat and run large basting stitches from side to side and from top to bottom to hold the layers together firmly. Machine up and down in the seams where the stencilled squares join and similarly from side to side. Finish the machine quilting by running a line of stitching around the border, 1 cm (⅜ in) from the edge of the squares. Remove the basting and make the ties into bows. Add some quilting knots to the border. Using double thread, take a stitch through all layers on the right side, leaving the loose ends long. Take a back stitch, bringing the needle out in the same place. Remove the needle, tie the loose ends into a knot and trim. Make six on each side and four each at the top and bottom.*

LEFT: *The finished quilt should be laundered carefully in hand-wash detergent. The French metal bed on which the quilt is displayed in this picture is a photographer's prop only and is not recommended for a young child to sleep in.*

NURSERY CUSHIONS

TEDDIES AND rabbits are amongst the most popular of motifs for children of all ages. Here they have been stencilled on cushions to decorate the nursery, although a little fabric ted found his way into the picture along with a tiny cupboard! Should you have a favourite teddy or toy in the house, try designing your own stencil to create a very personal and special nursery or child's bedroom (see page 16). Otherwise, use the templates on page 92 to cut stencils from plastic film.

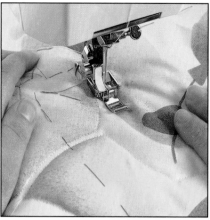

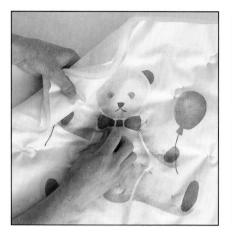

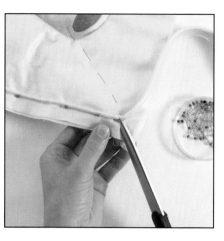

1 Wash and dry your fabric. Cut squares, circles or rectangles of fabric large enough to accommodate the chosen motif with a 1 cm (⅜ in) seam allowance added. Choose appropriate coloured fabric stencil paints and stencil the motifs onto the fabric, keeping the fabric taped down flat. Use the brush method (see page 18), keeping the stencil film in place with spray adhesive. Employ shading to add life and form to the teddies and rabbits, using a darker shade than the basic body colour. For a quilted cushion cover, place the stencilled fabric right side up over light-weight wadding and muslin. Pin and baste the three layers together with large stitches, starting at the centre each time and sewing to each corner and to the middle of each side.

2 Thread the sewing machine with cotton to match the stencil colouring. Fit the piping foot – this gives a good edge to run along the perimeter of the motif because the needle follows along the edge of the foot. Machine all around the motifs, picking out details for sewing around as well. Pull the ends through to the wrong side with a sewing needle and secure.

3 Make piping as described on page 21. Pin in place around the edges of the right side of the stencilled square, raw edges matching. Tack over pinning and machine in place. Remove the tacking, cut and lay the fabric back on top of the cushion front with right sides facing. Pin in place. Machine over previous stitching on three sides. Trim off excess fabric close to the piping, clip the corners and turn through to the right side. Insert a cushion pad and sew up the opening.

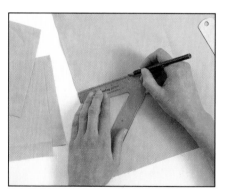

4 To make a nine-panelled cushion requires accuracy. Use a set square to ensure that corners are a true 90°. Mark the cutting line lightly with a pencil right across the fabric, then sub-divide this into 15 cm (6 in) squares. Stencil each square and join them down side seams in sets of three. Finally sew three rows together. Pipe and finish (see page 21) as for step 3.

5 For the walking teddy cushion, cut two stencils from clear plastic film (its transparency helps placement of the repeating pattern), using the template on page 92. Find the fabric centre by folding in half and centre the teddy 'body' on the fold. Stencil the body first using the brush method and fabric paints in honey and brown for shading. Then use the second stencil to fill in the details in brown paint, adding a red scarf. Stencil two more teddies to either side, marking the position of the previous teddy in permanent marker pen on the edges of the body stencil to help place the stencil correctly each time. Make up the cushion as for step 3.

LEFT: Mix images of various sizes to create interest and make objects from stencilled fabric that need occasional washing only (launder carefully in hand-wash detergent). Continue the nursery theme by stencilling other objects in the room. Here the teddies come to life marching across a pretty wall cupboard. Stencil them onto stripped and sanded wood (see page 12) and protect with furniture wax, buffed to a soft shine.

EGYPTIAN BATHROOM

THE BATHROOM is an often neglected room in the house. A sad thought when you consider how much time is spent in there relaxing in a hot bath. It takes very little time to create a peaceful haven – try stencilling on a plain blind or make a fabric shower curtain to hang decoratively outside the plastic waterproof variety. Even tiles can be stencilled successfully with a little help from a can of special varnish!

BELOW: *The blue, rag-rolled crenellation represents the Nile, which has plants growing on its banks and water containers waiting to be filled. The sphinxes are instantly recognizable while the flowers are a traditional ancient Egyptian motif.*

1 To echo the crenellated edge of the blind illustrated, find the centre and mark lightly with a pencil, then measure out to either side. Calculate the lengths of tape needed to form a channel 2.5 cm (1 in) wide with three evenly spaced crenellations. Run 2.5 cm (1 in) wide masking tape out onto a cutting board, and use its grid lines to cut the tape squarely and accurately. Stick two lines of tape onto the blind forming the channel. Mix up a blue glaze (see page 15), paint and rag roll the area between the tape (see step 4 of the Classic Rug on page 46).

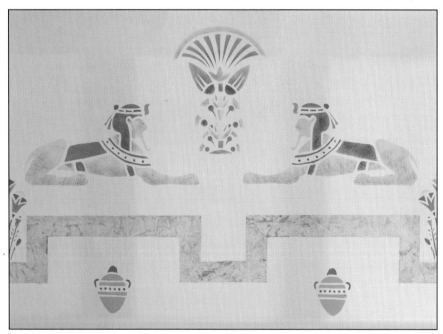

RIGHT: *On a large area like the shower curtain spread the motifs out well or you will be there all day stencilling! Do not pay too much attention to the top area of the blind either – most of the time it's rolled up.*

2 Cut palm tree, water carrier, flower and sphinx stencils (see page 16) using the templates on page 93. Work the design on the blind, using hard surface paints and the brush method (see page 18). Use strong shades of red, green, blue and yellow. Complete one half before reversing the stencils for other half. To clean the stencil before turning over, wet kitchen paper towel with cellulose thinners and carefully rub over the paint to dissolve it. Work in a well-ventilated room – the fumes can be unpleasant if inhaled.

3 To calculate the fabric required for the curtain, measure the height of the finished curtain and add 16 cm (6½ in) for turnings. Join widths if necessary. Turn in the selvedges to the wrong side and machine-sew. Along the top, turn down a double 4 cm (1½ in) hem and machine close to the fold. Repeat on the bottom. Count up the number of top rings needed and mark on the curtain top. Working on an old piece of wood with a small hammer, make eyelet holes with a purchased eyelet set. Stencil the curtain with fabric paints to match the blind, using the illustration as a guide.

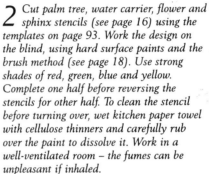

4 Tiles must be dry and free from any traces of grease or dust before stencilling. Wash down with sugar soap and dry well. Stencil using the brush method (see page 18) and hard surface paints in bright colours that are reminiscent of Egyptian designs. To colour in little areas of the stencil, it may be easier to abandon the stencil brush in favour of a stiff artist's brush.

5 Notice that the stencil does not have to be directly centred over the tile – these flowers have been positioned as though growing out of the base of the tile, as they are along the crenellated border on the blind. Protect your hard work with a coat of ceramic varnish, painting over the entire area of the tile.

CLASSIC RUG

IN TERMS OF decorating, the floor is generally forgotten or the last to be considered. Yet here is a huge expanse to be played with. Floor rugs are not only functional but decorative too. They look best set against plain floorboards, where the eye is naturally drawn to them. Apart from providing visual interest, they also help to insulate and keep a room warm by blocking out cold and draughts.

1 *This rug measures 70 x 136 cm (27 x 53 in). You will need a piece of heavy artist's canvas at least 20 cm (8 in) larger all around than the finished size. Press the canvas, then pin to a large sheet of board with upholstery tacks and a hammer. Start by tacking down at the middle of each side and work out towards the corners – do not hammer the tacks in fully.*

RIGHT: The simplicity of a classical design is hard to beat. The subtle colouring and geometry of the pattern fits in with most styles of decoration and blends well with furniture of all ages.

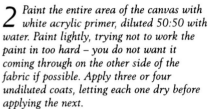

2 Paint the entire area of the canvas with white acrylic primer, diluted 50:50 with water. Paint lightly, trying not to work the paint in too hard – you do not want it coming through on the other side of the fabric if possible. Apply three or four undiluted coats, letting each one dry before applying the next.

3 Pull out the tacks and trim the edges off square using a steel rule, set square and sharp craft knife. Mark a line 2.5 cm (1 in) all around the edge and another, 5 cm (2½ in) inside that. Carefully trim off each corner close to the inner marked line. Turn cloth over to the wrong side. Fold in a hem along the first marked line and then along the second. Stick hems with PVA glue. Allow to dry. Sand smooth any cracks and paint the back with one coat of primer.

4 On the right side, lightly mark a line 8 cm (3 in) in from the edge all around and another 15 cm (6 in) inside that. Run masking tape on either side of these lines, making good, square corners. Mix up a pale green glaze (see page 15). Paint it between the lines of the tape. Immediately dampen a clean rag with white spirit, roll up and run over the glaze to partially remove it. Run tape around the outside edge and paint and rag roll between this and the previous tape. Also rag roll the central area with grey glaze. When dry, cut stencils of the two motifs from the templates on page 94 (see page 16) and stencil with a brush (see page 18) in shades of green, dark brown and tan, using hard surface paints. Seal with acrylic floor varnish.

SEA CREATURES DECK CHAIR

E VEN THE MOST hard-working of us need to relax sometime. Whether it is lazing on a sunny beach or out in the back garden, a comfortable, padded chair is essential. A coat of glistening new paint and newly-stencilled covers will transform a dingy old deck-chair. If you are lucky, you may find a deck-chair complete with footrest for putting your feet up as well – add a head pillow too and you will never go back to work!

1 Lay the chair and the footrest, if you have one, out flat, taking care not to catch your fingers in the frame. Carefully ease out the old tacks holding the fabric in place and keeping the old canvas as reference for sizing later. Remove the metal hooks from the footrest, storing them safely.

2 Remove any paint finish from the wood, following the directions on page 12. Sand down the wood and the metal hooks with glasspaper or wire wool until smooth. Purchase two cans of spray paint suitable for both wood and metal. These paints need no undercoating and dry quickly. If possible, hang the frame from an 'S' hook while painting it. Spray paint the wooden frames all over. If you have them, spray paint the footrest metal hooks.

3 Deckchair canvas is produced to fit the frames and has a selvedge down each side. However, the foot rest is usually slightly narrower than the chair and turnings must be taken. Use the old canvas pieces as a measurement for the new fabric length, cutting two pieces for the chair. Cut sea monster and fish stencils using the templates on page 95 (see page 16) and stencil one deckchair piece and the footrest with fabric stencil paints in red and green with yellow for the fish eyes, plus acrylic silver. Attach the canvas to the frame with 13 mm (⅝ in) upholsterer's nails and a magnetic-headed hammer.

4 Press the deckchair pieces if necessary and lay the stencilled piece the wrong side up and cover with the second piece. Pin down either side and machine together with buttonhole thread 1 cm (⅜ in) from the edge. Cut heavy-weight wadding 20 cm (8 in) shorter than the canvas and insert between the two pieces of fabric. Run two lines of basting, evenly spaced, down the length. Machine along these lines. Attach to the deck-chair frame as for the foot rest.

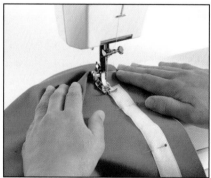

5 For the head pillow, cut two pieces of canvas 41 x 36 cm (16 x 14 in). Stencil one piece as before. Press to set the paint. Lay right side up with the second piece on top. Sew the sides and bottom edges, taking 1 cm (⅜ in) seams. Cut a piece of wadding that fits the width but that is 10 cm (4 in) shorter in depth. Cut a 36 cm (14 in) length of self-adhesive velcro. Stick one half to the back of the chair frame and sew the other half to the back of the top edge of the pillow back. Turn the pillow to the right side and insert the wadding. Turn in raw edges and slip stitch closed.

RIGHT: For an individual look on the beach, decorate bright, new canvas with fantastic sea monsters in lurid red and silver. Paint the wooden frame to match for a stunning co-ordinated look.

FRILLED SEAT COVERS

1 *Make a pattern of the missing seat from a sheet of newspaper. Tape the paper on firmly so that it does not slip. Using a steel rule and marker pen, gently feel for the inside edge of the seat and mark a line about 1 cm (⅜ in) outside this around the front and sides. Mark the curved back edge freehand. Cut around the marked lines with paper scissors.*

C LASSIC KITCHEN and dining room chairs like these dainty oak ones are easy to pick up cheaply, especially if, like these, the seats were missing. Originally the seats had been caned but this is expensive and time consuming to have re-done or try doing yourself. Although the loose weave of the caned finish is in keeping with the style of the chairs, adding pretty, frilled seat covers creates the same lightness of feel.

2 *Oak has a marked open grain which takes colouring or liming beautifully. Open the grain further with a large wire brush, rubbing firmly in the direction of the grain. Work out of doors if possible or wear a face mask as the dust produced is very fine. Work into the corners with a shoe suede brush. This should remove all traces of the original finish or varnish.*

3 *Brush off any dust left from the wirebrushing and rub over the chairs with a clean rag, dampened in white spirit. Stain with purchased coloured wood dye in apple green, following the directions in step 4 on page 31. Use the paper seat pattern to cut new seat boards from 5 mm (⅕ in) thick plywood, using an electric jigsaw or cutting by hand with a fretsaw. Sand the edges smooth with glass paper and position over the chair. Hold in place with 13 mm (½ in) bronzed upholsterer's nails. Start in the centre of each side and work into the corners.*

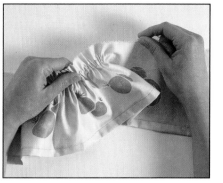

ABOVE: Make a feature of two chairs by standing them either side of a cupboard tinted the same colour. Add a matching cloth, set jauntily at an angle, or some vegetable-covered cushions.

4 From 120 cm (48 in) wide cream fabric, cut two 13 cm (5 in) deep pieces the width of the fabric for the frill. Sew together down one short edge, right sides facing. Cut cabbage, tomato, carrot and bean stencils (see page 16) using the templates on page 96. Use a brush (see page 18) to stencil the right side of the frill with tomatoes, using fabric stencil paints in red, green and white. On the bottom edge, turn up a double 1.5 cm (½ in) hem and machine sew. On the top edge, machine sew double lines of long stitches, breaking off and starting again every 60 cm (24 in). Pull up the stitching to gather.

5 Make a pattern of the seat, adding a 1 cm (⅜ in) seam all around. Cut two seat pieces from cream fabric. Stencil one with vegetables. Make 150 cm (59 in) of contrast piping (see page 21) in burnt orange and sew all around the stencilled front piece. Cover the piping on the sides and front edge with the gathered frill, matching raw edges. Machine in place. Place the back piece over the front with right sides facing and with the frill tucked inside. Machine in place leaving the back edge open.

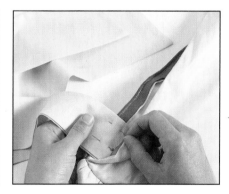

6 Trim away the excess fabric around the sides and front edges. Clip at the corners right up to the stitching line and around any curves. Cut medium-weight wadding to fit inside the seat. Turn the seat to the right side and press well, setting the paint following the manufacturer's instructions. Slip the wadding inside.

7 Cut four 60 x 20 cm (24 x 8 in) pieces of cream fabric for ties. Fold in half down the length of each one and machine along one short edge and along the long edge, tapering the stitching away from the raw edge to form a narrow open end measuring 5 cm (2 in). Trim away excess fabric and turn to the right side. Pin and machine the narrow ends of two ties over the piping in both corners of the open back edge. Machine over previous stitching. Turn in the raw edges of the seat and slip stitch closed. Place on the chair, tying bows around the back struts.

FLORAL CUPBOARD

THIS 1930S utility-type cupboard in its original coat of drab brown varnish might well have been overlooked in the furniture area of a second-hand store had it not had reams of storage space and, more importantly, those lovely flat panelled doors. These instantly spelled potential. They could have remained a large uninterrupted area on which to stencil but cutting out gothic openings seemed more exciting.

RIGHT: A matching cushion (see steps 1–3 of the Nursery Cushions on page 42) complements the stencil design shown on the cupboard. Each piece of fabric for the cupboard doors has six rose motifs stencilled in a regular pattern over it. Use stencil crayons for the fabric as they are easy to work with. Leave to dry before making up and launder by hand – do not dry clean.

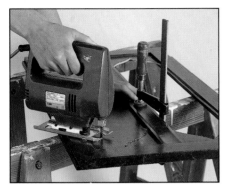

1 Remove the doors, keeping hinges, gripper hooks and screws in a safe place. Draw a gothic arch on paper, the width of the panel, and cut out. Use this template to mark the top and bottom of each panel. Secure the door to working trestles. Drill a couple of pilot holes at the widest point of the arch for the blade of an electric jigsaw to fit into and, using the jigsaw, carefully cut out the entire shape. Your local carpenter will do this for you if you do not own or cannot hire a jigsaw from a tool hire store.

2 To create your own design , use tracing paper and a fine permanent marking pen to trace off flowers and leaves at random from a piece of patterned fabric. Try to run the pen around whole areas of colour each time, creating areas that can be cut out later from stencil card. If there seem to be too many little areas, join a few together to make larger ones and simplify the design. Use your drawing to cut out a stencil (see page 16). Otherwise, use the template on page 97 to cut a stencil of the rose motif illustrated here.

3 Remove any handles and sand down the entire cupboard with glasspaper wrapped around a sanding block. Fill any holes with fine surface filler and paint with primer and two top coats of pale pink eggshell. Make up a deep pink glaze (see page 15). Mask off the edges of the drawers, paint on the glaze and sponge (see step 2, page 61). Remove the masking tape When dry, mask off again to leave a line a line around the sponge work. Paint in the line with the glaze. Paint a line around the sides of the cupboard in the same way. Paint and sponge the glaze on the door surrounds. Using part of the stencil cut in step 2, stencil the rose motif at each end of the cupboard drawers and at each corner of the sides of the cupboard using pink and green stencil crayons (see page 19).

4 To complement this cupboard's new Victorian gothic look, the very 1930s handles were replaced with traditional wooden knobs. Paint them using the same colour as for the main cupboard. Add a line of glaze around the base of each one. Dry carefully. Cut a rosebud stencil from the template on page 97. Hold it firmly in place with your fingers – it will not stick with spray adhesive – while stencilling with pink and green hard surface paints and a stencil brush (see page 18).

BELOW: To calculate fabric amounts needed, measure the door width and multiply by two and a half. If possible use the whole width of the fabric with selvedges at either side as they need no hemming and add no bulk.

5 To attach the stencilled fabric to the doors you will require 9 mm (⅜ in) diameter dowelling, small screw eyes and small brass drawer knobs. Measure the width of the fabric openings on each door and add 2 cm (¾ in). Cut four dowelling pieces this length. To fit the knobs, make holes at both ends of each dowelling piece with an electric drill. Secure the dowelling in a vice while drilling slowly and carefully.

6 Measure the height of the panel for the fabric curtain and add 10 cm (4 in). Stencil the fabric with pink and green oil-based crayons and a brush (see page 19, keeping the stencil in place with spray adhesive and positioning the motif in a regular pattern on the fabric. Allow to dry. Take a double 2.5 cm (1 in) hem along the top and bottom raw edges for a dowel channel, leaving the selvedges at the sides. Machine hem. Using the dowel as a guide, position a screw eye level at each end of the top and bottom of both doors. Slip the fabric channel over the dowel, place between the eyes and secure with brass knobs. Replace the doors on the cupboard.

ABOVE: Use only part of the stencil on the drawers. Mask off the areas you will not be painting with masking tape. Stencil beyond the 'lining' and under where the knob is positioned to add visual interest.

DECORATIVE EFFECTS

Use stencilling to play decorative tricks on walls, floors and furniture. Mosaics, tiles, frosted and patterned glass can all be imitated to stunning effect while *trompe l'oeil* shelves, windows and garden screens will delight and amuse your friends.

TILED WALL

ALTHOUGH ceramic tiles might be practical in a kitchen or bathroom, they would be expensive and time-consuming to put up elsewhere. Adding fake tiles can look just as effective at a fraction of the cost. Try stencilling them onto a plain wall in a hall. The addition of a dado rail makes the tiles look all the more realistic. For use in a steamy atmosphere like the kitchen, paint over the tiles when dry with polyurethane varnish – a gloss variety will look just like glaze.

1 If you have a favourite tile design that you would like to replicate, try making up your own stencil, following the instructions on page 16. Keep to a standard size – 10 cm (4 in) and 15 cm (6 in) square are most often used. For a two-colour tile, or one containing several elements, you will need to divide the motif into two stencils. Otherwise, use the template provided on page 97 of the tile design illustrated here. For this design, the background ribbon was first traced and cut out on stencil card while the main floral motif was traced onto a separate piece of card and cut out (see pages 16–17).

RIGHT: Stencilled tiles are an inexpensive decorative feature for large areas of wall in the house and have the added advantage of never cracking! Create a period look by copying Victorian tiles or use contemporary ideas to inspire your theme.

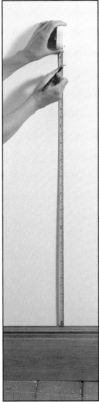

3 Trim the stencil card very close to the top of the background ribbon edge. This allows the card to fit flush against the wall right up to the dado. Stick masking tape along the top edge to protect the dado from the paint. To aid registration, draw in a continuation of the wall lines onto the stencil card. Stencil with oil-based crayons (see page19) for speed over a large area, using green amd dark blue shades. Secure the stencils to the wall with spray adhesive. Clean your brushes afterwards in white spirit and soap and water.

2 Having established the tile size, measure up from the skirting board, allowing for five 15 cm (6 in) square tiles under a dado rail for the design illustrated here. Allow for 'grouting' too – 3 mm (1/8 in) between each tile and at the top and bottom. Attach the dado rail, gluing and screwing it in place. Using a plumbline and a pencil, mark the vertical lines of grouting with a set square and rule. Mark horizontal lines to represent the tiles and grouting.

4 Leave the stencil to dry, a process that may take several days. Add a realistic touch with a shadow line, deciding on the direction of the main light source in the hall or room and therefore which side of the tile the shadow should lie. There should be a shadow line under the tile as well. Cut a narrow shadow line stencil and apply a soft grey shadow with hard-surface stencil paint.

GEOMETRIC PATIO & POTS

CONSERVATORY or patio paving and containers are often left undecorated, but they cry out to be painted with stencils to elevate them from the humble and hum-drum. Take the classical theme even further by stencilling the walls with the mosiac motif and concealing garden statuary among your plants. Decorate planters and containers in complementary style with bold geometric lines, inventing your own designs to add a personal creative touch.

RIGHT: Old or tired-looking tiles can be given a new lease of life with a simple stencil. The mosaic motif illustrated here is reminiscent of Roman decoration and is ideally suited to a conservatory. Leave the main thoroughfare undecorated as the paint will wear off very quickly or give the floor several coats of varnish to protect it.

MOSAIC TILES

1 Use the templates on page 98 to cut stencils from clear plastic film (see page 16) for the border and corner squares. Trace and cut out the central green squares for both border and corners on a separate sheet of film. Using a stencil brush (see page 18) and red and black hard-surface stencil paints, stencil a border of red and black squares. Use the transparency of the film to position it over the matching end of the length you have just painted in order to keep your border straight. Position the centre stencil between them and stencil in green. Stencil each corner, using the illustration as a guide for positioning and painting the black and red squares first. Mask off the colour not being painted to avoid mistakes. Position the central squares and stencil in green.

2 Use the template on page 98 to cut a quarter circle stencil from a square of clear plastic film (see page 16). This template was designed to fit tiles 29 cm (11½ in) square but it can be reduced or enlarged on a photocopier to fit your own tiles. Align the edges of the stencil with those of the tile and stencil in red and black, masking off the colour not being used as before.

RIGHT: Plain watering cans and pots may be fine for the garden, but in a conservatory they can be livened up with strong geometric stencil designs that complement the classical mosaic tiles.

ALUMINIUM POT

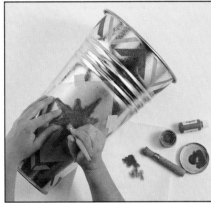

1 *When stencilling around curved objects, simple designs and designs made up from several repeating elements work best of all. Use the templates on page 98 to cut star and border design stencils from clear plastic film (see page 16). On metallic curved surfaces such as this, it is necessary to tape the stencil film down extra firmly. Spray adhesive may also be necessary on the reverse of the stencil. Hold down the points of the stars if necessary. Stencil the star motif using a brush (see page 18) and red hard-surface paints. Stencil the triangular border motifs using red and gold paints. Decorate any raised bands on the pot with lines of green paint.*

WATERING CAN

 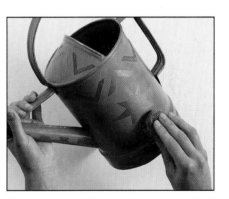

1 *Use glasspaper to sand the watering can smooth. Remove any rust and paint with red oxide primer. Paint in a top coat of green eggshell. When dry, use the same stencils and paints as for the aluminium pot and stencil in red and gold to match. Add a gold 'lining' around any raised rims, using gold acrylic paint and a medium-sized artist's brush. Hold the can steady while you work. As the paintbrush is run along, a finger of the same hand runs parallel along the rim, acting as a measure and a steadier.*

2 *To give the watering can a fashionable antique feel, rub off some of the decoration and the top coat with fine grade wire wool. Concentrate on areas that would rub off naturally, like the handle and sides.*

FRENCH
BREAD BIN

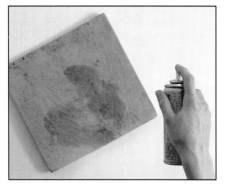

1 *After stripping the bin back to the bare wood (see page 12), check for any signs of woodworm in the form of little holes, as though made by a thumb tack. In the spring, any patches of wood dust are a tell-tale sign of woodworm. Spray well with a proprietary brand of woodworm killer. Flatten a warped lid by laying between damp newspapers under a heavy weight until it has dried. Repeat if necessary.*

W HEN IT COMES to food and design, the French always seem to come up with something unusual and functional. A tall wooden bin to store their long sticks of bread is no exception. Its flat surfaces are very appealing to the stenciller but do require some ingenuity to fill the tall shape. Hence the cat sitting in the window.

ABOVE: Position the stencil carefully, so that the mouse sits in front of the pot, with his tail hanging over the edge of the windowsill. Add individual hairs, whiskers and highlights to eyes with an artist's brush.

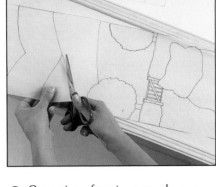

2 *Cover the bin with several layers of eggshell paint in pale cream and allow to dry. To create the background sponged effect, mix an oil-based glaze (see page 15). It looks best as a darker shade of the base colour. Paint the glaze over areas that are not being stencilled. Dampen a natural sponge with white spirit and dab all over the glaze to partially remove it. Clean the sponge regularly with more white spirit.*

3 *Cut a piece of tracing paper the same size as the panel to be stencilled. Using the templates on page 99, draw in a windowsill at the bottom and draw the cat sitting on it to one side. Sketch in the hedge, trees and hills in the background, lengthening or shortening them to fit your bin. Cover with another piece of tracing and draw in the main outlines only. Cut out the different elements carefully with paper scissors.*

4 *Using the original drawing as a guide, place the cut-out templates in position on the front panel and draw around their outside edges with a soft pencil. The raised edge on the front of this bin acted as a natural frame for the stencilled picture. On the sides of the bin a margin of a few centimetres was left all around the 'picture', to echo the front raised edge.*

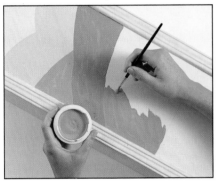

5 *Little pots of emulsion paint are ideal for painting in the background and the garden. Buy two greens and a blue. Mix together a small amount from both pots of green to create another shade and use to paint in the hills and the foreground. Remember, the farthest hill will be the palest. Add sky. The eggshell paint forms the blind background and the sill. Paint the tartan blind with lines of red, using a square-ended artist's brush, and lines of green, using a fine brush. Paint in birds in grey.*

LEFT: *A French bread bin is equally at home in any kitchen. Pick the base colour to match or tone with your existing units and keep it pale – it will need to be painted over by lots of other shades.*

6 *Cut a stencil for the tree/hedge and gate. Dampen in water a natural sponge with open holes. Thin a little stencil paint in a darker green than the hills. Dip the sponge into the paint and clean off any excess onto kitchen paper. Dab lightly through the stencil to form trees and a hedge. Note that the stencil has open edges; mask well here. Stencil the gate and tree trunks in brown hard-surface paints, using the brush method (see page 18).*

7 *'Paint' apples on the trees, using a large stencil brush. Dip the bristles into red stencil paint but do not remove the excess paint as usual. Press the brush firmly down to produce a circle or spot. Add highlights in white. Stencil the cat using the template as a reference and paint in the details by hand. Use a fine artist's brush and stencil paints to add whiskers, hair, and highlights to the eyes (see page 12). Continue the hills, hedge, trees and blind on the sides. Cut stencils of the mouse and pot of chives (see pages 16–17). Stencil the pot on each side in terracotta, brown and two shades of green and purple. Stencil the mouse on one side only. Colour him in two shades of brown, with pink ears and nose and black eyes. Add highlights in white to the eyes and additional hairs in brown and white (see page 12).*

CHILD'S DRESSER

ECORATING anything in miniature is always appealing. It is not only the small scale that is fascinating but the memories of childhood that are conjured up too. The previous owner of this child's dresser had started work on restoring it, but sadly had given up halfway through. Panels had been added at the sides to hide some defect and were removed to show a very damaged base, probably due to being stored somewhere damp.

1 Add interest to the little doors using moulding. Mark the outside edge position of the moulding with a pencil. Carefully measure and cut pieces of moulding to the appropriate lengths, using a 45° mitre block and a fine, sharp saw. Each length is mitred at both ends with the cut angled away from the inside to the outside. Spread the underside of each length with wood glue.

2 Position the glue-backed moulding pieces onto the door, placing the outside edges on the pencil lines. Press down firmly and remove any glue that seeps out with a damp cloth. Pin the moulding in place, using a small hammer and 20 mm (¾ in) panel pins. Fill in any gaps or defects at the mitred corners with fine surface filler using a filler knife.

3 Moisture had started to lift up the top layers of the plywood sides along the bottom edge of this dresser. Cutting a curve at this point not only removed some of the damaged area but also added interest to the plain side. Mark a shallow curve with a pencil and carefully cut along it with a sharp fret saw. Fill where necessary with fine surface filler and sand smooth the entire dresser and the doors with glasspaper.

4 Paint the entire dresser with pink eggshell paint and allow to dry. In a wide-mouthed glass jar, mix up a strong coloured glaze (see page 15) made from a touch of white eggshell paint, artist's oil in ultramarine, and white spirit. Paint one side only, using a household decorating brush removing any drips that form on the edges.

RIGHT: *Pink and blue are the obvious colours for a little girl's dresser, but you can choose a colour scheme to match it with its surroundings. On the back of the shelves stencil books, plates, a seated doll and a ted.*

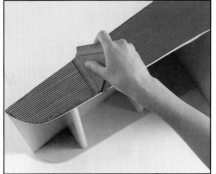

5 Immediately, take a rubber comb and run gently but firmly in a straight line from one end to the other. Repeat the process until the whole side has a pattern of lines on it. Clean the excess paint off the comb with a clean rag each time a line of combing is completed. Repeat the process of combing in the opposite direction to form a grid effect. If a mistake occurs, clean the glaze off with white spirit on a rag and repeat.

6 Pick out the moulding, the door handles, the edges of the side pieces and the front edges of the shelves with the same blue glaze. Paint on with care and remove any drips with white spirit on a clean rag. Allow the glaze to almost dry, then wipe over it with a white spirit-dampened rag so that some of the glaze is removed. Comb the outer area outside the moulding on the doors.

LEFT: A dresser is the perfect place for a small girl to store all her treasures, pretty doll's china and little books. The doors were removed for painting and stencilling and were rehung on the original brass and copper hinges which polished up beautifully. New handles were painted to match the blue edging.

7 Use the templates on page 100 to cut a standing and a sitting rag doll stencil, a teddy, a plate, a cup and saucer and a books stencil (see pages 16–17). Stencil the motifs over the shelves and onto the doors, using hard surface paints and the brush method (see page 18). You will need two or three shades of blue, green, red and tan paints, plus black for the rag doll's facial features and shoes. To stencil a rag doll facing in both directions, clean the paint off the used side of the stencil with cellulose thinners in a well-ventilated room, turn over and stencil on the other side. When the stencilling is dry, clean or replace the hinges and handles and rehang the doors.

GARDEN SCREEN

NLESS YOU are guaranteed beautiful weather all year round, when it is always possible to step out into the garden, it is a pleasant idea to bring a little of the garden indoors. A screen is the perfect medium for this as, stencilled with a garden motif, it can grace any room from a conservatory to a bedroom. Use it to disguise unsightly views or purely as a decorative room divider.

2 *Join several sheets of stencil card together to cover the area of one panel. Trace the container template on page 101 onto the bottom of the card. Draw in a topiary tree approximately 75 cm (29½ in) in height, following the illustration as a guide and leaving stencilling bridges (see page 16) between the trunk and the foliage. Add climbing ivy down one side. If you do not feel your drawing is up to it, pick various-sized ivy leaves from your own or a friend's garden and use them to trace around, making a random pattern. Leave a bridge down the middle of some leaves to indicate veining. Cut out your stencil and position it on one outside panel with spray adhesive. To recreate the texture of a topiary bush, use a sponge (see page 18) to apply several shades of green hard-surface paint on top of one another, keeping the colour denser down one side of the tree and at its base. Stencil the trunk in mid brown.*

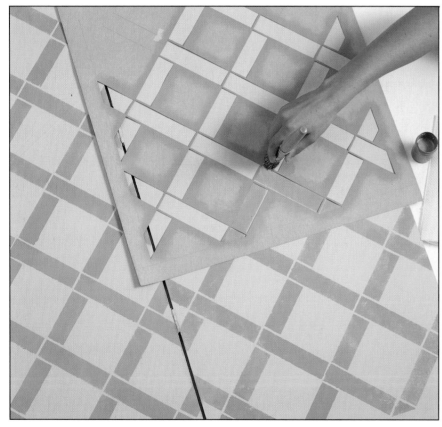

1 *Measure the dimensions of your screen and, on a large piece of stencil card, mark the width of the screen panels. Use the template on page 101 to trace and cut out an area of trellis stencil within the marked width (see page 16), following the illustration as a guide. Starting approximately 18 cm (7 in) from the bottom* *of your screen, stencil the trellis in soft brown hard-surface paint unevenly applied using a stencil brush (see page 18). Register the stencil by laying the centre bottom slats over the trellis peak you have just painted. Match up the slats at the sides of each panel, but do not worry if you cannot do this exactly.*

3 Paint the container in terracotta, using the brush method (see page 18) and lightly speckling small areas in a darker brown on a sponge. Stencil a second tree, omitting the smallest ball at the top. Use the templates on page 101 to cut a pot stencil and position it between the two trees. Stencil the pots in the same colours used for the topiary tree container, again speckling the pots with a darker brown paint applied with a sponge. Use the brush method to paint the herb leaves in green, adding touches of yellow and brown. Use a grey-green paint for the leaves of the sage and stencil the flower heads in purple with touches of red.

4 Cut out stencils for the hanging basket and the butterfly using the templates on page 101. Stencil the basket mesh in brown, unevenly applied with a brush. Use several shades of green with touches of brown and yellow to stencil the trailing geraniums leaves, and light green, grey and yellow for the tradescantia leaves. Draw veins on some of the leaves with a brown permanent marker pen. Stencil the geranium flowers in shades of red, using white highlights. Mix red and white for one flower to create pink geranium heads. Stencil the allium in yellow. Use yellow, red, blue and dark brown paints to stencil the butterfly.

LEFT: The same topiary tree stencil is used on two panels of the screen, but instant variation in height is achieved by shortening one of the trees. Move the ivy leaf stencil around at various angles to stencil a constantly differing arrangement of leaves. Place the basket in different positions and fill any gaps on the ground with herb pots.

FROSTED DOOR PANELS

S ADLY, PLAIN featureless doors are common in many houses. Being perfectly flat they are crying out to be stencilled, but a radical facelift before stencilling will transform them even more. Creating panels not only adds character, it restricts the stencilled decoration to a specific area making it visually much stronger. Inserting glass in the top panels adds another dimension, providing a different surface to work on and giving a totally new effect.

RIGHT: Having created a period-style door, look out for an art nouveau finger plate and a large brass knob. Decorate the door frame as though it were made from joined pieces of wood by painting with a deep pink glaze and dragging it.

LEFT: *Decorated glass to complement your decorating them is easy to achieve. Refer to art books for inspiration for your pattern, whether art nouveau, floral or geometric.*

1 *Measure and draw four rectangular panels onto a plain door with a flat surface. Leave the largest widths of frame at the bottom of the door, on a level with the handle, and down the centre. The width at the top of the frame and down either side should be slightly narrower. With a wood bit in an electric drill, make holes in each corner of each panel. Slip the blade of the jigsaw into a hole and carefully cut out each oblong-shaped panel. If you do not have a jigsaw, rent one from a tool hire store, or a carpenter can cut the panels for you.*

2 *Cut eight pieces of 15 mm (⅝ in) beading to fit each opening – four for the front of the door and four for the back. Tack all the front beading in place, using a hammer and 20 mm (¾ in) panel pins. Make sure the outermost edge of the beading sits level with the front plane of the door. The back beading will fit similarly later.*

3 *Having fitted the front beading, hold the back beading in place to calculate the thickness of glass or plywood needed to fit the gap that is left. If you cannot get an exact fit, the back beading will need to be fitted slightly deeper into the panel opening. Cut plywood pieces for bottom panels and fix in place with the beading and 20 mm (¾ in) panel pins. Sand down paintwork on the door with glasspaper, clean off dust with white spirit on a rag and paint in a pale shade of pink. Paint the entire surface of the door front with a deep pink glaze (see page 15) as quickly as possible. With a dragging brush pull through the glaze, starting and finishing where the joins would be in a period door. With a rag dampened in white spirit, clean stray glaze from the beading.*

4 *Stencilling is usually done by applying paint through holes. To create a frosted glass effect, it is the cut-out pieces from the 'holes' that are used. Trace the art nouveau motif template on page 102 onto two pieces of card the same size as your panels. Remember to allow for the depth of the beading around the edge. Lengthen or shorten the design as necessary. Cut out the art nouveau design on both pieces of card with a scalpel or sharp craft knife, making the edges as smooth as possible.*

5 *Keep the cut-out pieces carefully in a clear plastic folder. Have two glass panels cut to fit by a glazier. Place one over the original tracing of the motif. Trace the design out again on paper as a mirror image of the first. Place the second glass panel over it. Lay them side by side for working. Use spray adhesive to position the back of each cut-out piece on the glass over its counterpart on the drawing below. Press down firmly.*

6 *Paint the entire surface with clear, polyurethane matt vanish. If possible, use a new can of matt varnish and a clean brush. Any dust that settles on the wet varnish can spoil the finished, frosted effect. Run over the varnish with a clean, fluff-free roller. It will whiten or 'frost' the varnish. When dry, repeat twice more. Alternatively, spray three or four times with satin varnish, allowing it to dry between each application. Remove the cut-outs with great care when the varnish is dry. Clean away any glue with a cotton-wrapped stick dipped in lighter fuel. Fit the glass into the panel openings and fix as for the plywood pieces. Stencil the plywood pieces with a brush (see page 18), using the stencils created when cutting the pieces for frosting.*

COUNTRY CUPBOARD

IN NATURAL, waxed pine, this wall cupboard looked good in the farmhouse kitchen from where it was bought. But taken out of its old country setting it needed special treatment to give it back some life. Hence the bright, strong colours and the dramatic crackle finish. The country feel was retained in the simple stencilling on the glass doors.

BELOW: The entire cupboard was painted burgundy inside and out, then the lime green and crackle glazing were added to the top, sides and handles only as a contrast. Varnish with clear, matt polyurethane to add protection.

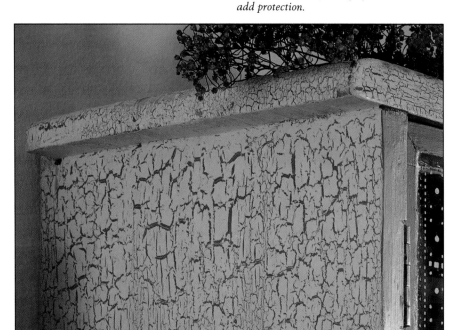

1 Remove the doors and take off the hinges before preparing the wood (see page 12). Keep the hinges and screws safely. Screws on old furniture are often difficult to remove, as these were. If the top of the screw is worn flat, try gently hammering the end of the screwdrive, so that its point is forced into the metal for a better grip. Spray with penetrating oil to loosen if all else fails.

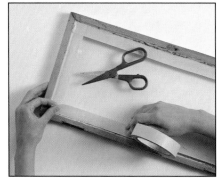

2 Strip off any old wax finish with methylated spirits and medium grade wire wool. Place the cupboard or door on plenty of newspaper while doing this to absorb the dirty methylated spirits. Clean the glass. Mask both sides of the glass, ready for painting.

3 Cover the whole cupboard and doors with two coats of burgundy matt emulsion paint. Leave to dry. The 'stencil' used here was part of a soft, plastic tablecloth, probably from the fifties, which had a perforated lacy pattern on it. A piece of old lace fabric or paper doily would do as well. Mount your 'stencil' onto the outside of the glass door using spray adhesive. Stencil using white hard surface paint and the brush method (see page 18).

LEFT: *If necessary, the stencilled glass can be cleaned very gently, using cotton-wool wrapped sticks soaked in lighter fuel. Try not to wet the stencil paint. Alternatively, varnish with clear gloss polyurethane to create a wipe-clean surface.*

4 To achieve the crackle effect, dissolve 1 kilo (1 pound) of gum arabic crystals (from good art stores) in 1.5 litres (2–3 pints) of cold water heated up in an old saucepan until they become the consistency of single or light cream. Strain, if necessary, through a sieve and cool before use. Store in a jar with a lid.

5 Paint the gum arabic solution over the top and sides and handles of the cupboard. Leave overnight to dry when the cracks will be clearly visible. With a wide brush, paint on the topcoat of lime green matt emulsion. The entire area to be crackled must be done quickly, with no attempt made to overbrush any part already painted or the cracks will vanish before your eyes. Leave to dry and re-attach the doors.

ACCESSORIES

The home would be
a very barren place indeed without lots of ornaments
to provide interest and decoration. Anything from
lampshades to letter racks can be adorned with
stencilling to sit in pride of place in your own home or
to be given as a unique gift to a special person.

VICTORIAN FIRE SCREEN

DURING the summer when the fire is not lit, the fireplace can be a gaping hole in the wall. Filled with a decorative screen and fresh plants it can be used as a focal point in the room. This 1930s screen was desperately in need of cheering up. Once painted and stencilled, it was transformed into a useful and striking accessory for the home.

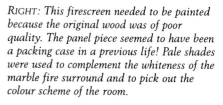

RIGHT: *This firescreen needed to be painted because the original wood was of poor quality. The panel piece seemed to have been a packing case in a previous life! Pale shades were used to complement the whiteness of the marble fire surround and to pick out the colour scheme of the room.*

1 Some of the varnishes used in the thirties become very thick and sticky when coated with paint stripper – this was one of them! Wear protective rubber gloves and use lots of medium grade wire wool to remove it. The wool will become clogged very quickly so replace frequently and re-apply stripper if required. Allow to dry and sand down well (see page 12).

2 Paint the entire screen in off-white oil-based paint. If time is short, use an acrylic primer for an undercoat as this dries almost immediately. Oil-based and acrylic paints may be used indiscriminately together. When dry, cover the panel area with green oil-based paint. On a dark object such as this, you will need to apply at least three coats in total to cover.

3 Add decorative touches reminiscent of the thirties. Sponging in gold was a favourite in those thrifty times as it made an object appear more luxurious than it really was. Use thinned acrylic gold paint, dabbing it on the edges only with a small natural sponge dampened in water. Use the templates on page 106 to cut stencils from plastic film for the Victorian lady, the flower, the tree and the crazy paving. Using the brush method (see page 18), stencil the lady in shades of pink, white, blue and cream hard-surface paints. Use brown, green and mauve paints to paint the remaining stencils. To stencil in reverse, clean the used side of the stencil with cellulose thinner in a well-ventilated room and turn over.

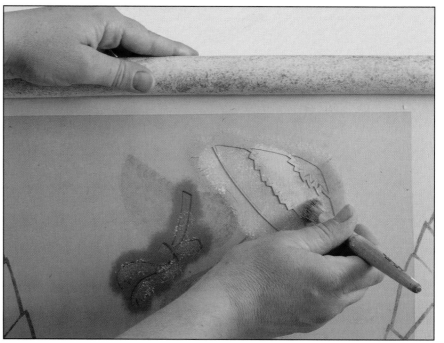

4 One of the beauties of stencilling is the facility of mixing colours on the stencil itself to give shading. This can create the impression of roundness, for example. On the lady's dress and umbrella stencil white over pink on the left hand side as a highlight and add a darker pink on the other side to produce shadowing.

IVY-LEAF
TIE-BACK

I F STENCILLING a whole curtain sounds a little daunting, try making tie-backs first. They are a quick and easy accessory to make from scraps of fabric left over from soft furnishing projects. Alternatively, make them in a toning colour, as shown here, or use a contrasting fabric for dramatic effect.

BELOW: If the brush is still wet after stencilling the tie-back fabric, continue the pattern along the wall to create a dado! A small repeating design like this breaks up a flat, coloured wall beautifully.

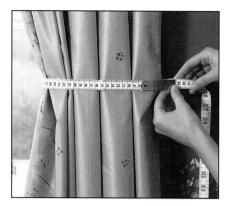

1 LEFT: *Plain ready-made curtains are ideal subjects for stencilling. Here the main motif is stencilled on the inside border edge and the remaining area covered with a tiny pattern of berries. Use the template on page 102 to cut an ivy leaf stencil from plastic film (see page 16). Stencil with fabric paints in soft green, green, red, yellow, orange and white, using the brush method (see page 18). Keep the stencil in place on the fabric with spray adhesive. For the tie-back, measure around your curtain with a tape measure to find the length of fabric required. Add 3 cm (1⅛ in) hem allowance.*

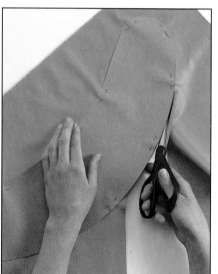

2 *Halve the tie-back measurement. Draw onto folded paper the outline of a curved tie-back to this measurement. Cut out and open. Use this pattern to cut two pieces of fabric and a lining of heavy-weight stiffening. Use the template on page 102 to cut a stencil from the ivy leaf and berries motif (see page 16). Stencil onto the right side of the front tie-back piece, using red, yellow, orange and green fabric paints and referring to the brush stencilling method on page 18. Make a length of piping in a darker or contrasting colour and machine sew around the edges of the front piece on the right side (see page 21). Cover on the right side with the lining and back piece. Sew around the edge, leaving a gap for turning. Trim the raw edges and clip the curves, turn to the right side and sew the opening closed. Sew a metal ring to the wrong side of each end of each tie-back and attach tie-back hooks to the wall.*

GINGHAM SHELF EDGING

Simple to make, shelf edging transforms plain cupboards and dressers in the kitchen, creating a sense of unity between shelves displaying a variety of items. The colour scheme used here will suit most kitchens but you may prefer to pick a colour that either tones with that of the objects you are displaying or one that reflects the colour scheme used in your kitchen.

RIGHT: Position the shelf edging just below the top edge of the shelf so that a neat line of wood is visible. This adds to the overall decorative effect. Replace the fabric lining with another paper one, or even add a third layer if the distance between the shelves is very great.

BELOW: Make a double-layered edging, backing the stencilled paper with fabric. Here the geometric design of the wallpaper is matched with similarly patterned gingham.

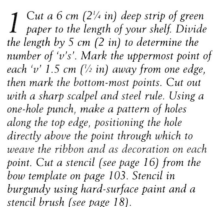

1 Cut a 6 cm (2¼ in) deep strip of green paper to the length of your shelf. Divide the length by 5 cm (2 in) to determine the number of 'v's'. Mark the uppermost point of each 'v' 1.5 cm (½ in) away from one edge, then mark the bottom-most points. Cut out with a sharp scalpel and steel rule. Using a one-hole punch, make a pattern of holes along the top edge, positioning the hole directly above the point through which to weave the ribbon and as decoration on each point. Cut a stencil (see page 16) from the bow template on page 103. Stencil in burgundy using hard-surface paint and a stencil brush (see page 18).

2 Choose a closely-woven green gingham fabric for the shelf edging lining; otherwise it will fray badly when cut. Press onto the reverse side of the fabric a length of light-weight iron-on interfacing as used in dressmaking. Cut as for the paper, marking the uppermost point of the 'v' 3 cm (1⅛ in) from the top edge of the fabric and the bottommost points 7.5 cm (3 in) away. Cut out carefully with pinking shears. Thread the holes along the top of the paper with three lengths of fine burgundy ribbon, one in the centre section and the others to either side. Secure with glue at the outer edges. Tie the loose ends in bows. Glue the gingham edging to the back of the paper with general purpose adhesive. Secure on the shelf with double-sided sticky tape.

DECORATIVE LIGHTING

UNUSUAL AND interesting lighting provides one of the best finishing touches to a room. Transform bought shades with decorative and pretty stencilling, or try making your own from coloured card to match your decor. The old-fashioned style of candle lamp with card shade is back in fashion and does not even need electricity. Or give a new lease of life to an old lamp simply by stencilling the shade.

COLUMN BASE

1 An attractive shape covered in layers and layers of paint, this base looked even better after stripping, when the moulding was given back its original definition. Paint the base with stripper and leave to work before rubbing with fine wire wool. Use the wool to work into the grooves. Wear rubber gloves and repeat several times if you need to.

2 After stripping with wire wool, the base may not even need sanding. Wipe off any traces of paint with white spirit on a clean rag (see page 12). Paint with red fontenay paste (from good art stores). Allow to dry for a few hours before painting with gilt cream. Gilt cream is available in various shades of gold and in a silver and pewter version. The gold varieties look best over a red base, while the silvery ones need a black undercoat. Use a stiff-bristled brush to push the cream well into the grooves.

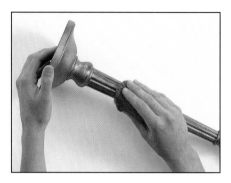

3 Leave the gilt cream for twelve hours to dry. Then sand off gently with fine wire wool in 0000 grade. Try to remove the gilt in places where wear would have naturally occurred.

4 Patinating, or ageing, is done with gilt patina pencils. These are usually purchased in packs of three, each a slightly different colour. Use them after buffing up the gilt cream, just as though they were coloured crayons. If you want to 'antique' or add years to a gilded item, these will do it instantly. Paint a metal shade with copper spray paint and stencil both the base and shade with the small leaf motif and border leaf motifs, using the templates on page 104 to cut stencils from clear plastic film. Use red and pale green hard-surface paints and the brush method (see page 18).

BAISE BASES

New baise bases are often necessary when renovating lamps. They can be cut from red or green self-adhesive flocked vinyl covering.

CANDLE LAMP

1 Chip any old wax from the base with your fingernail if possible – a blade will mark the wood. Sand off any last traces of wax with coarse wire wool and remove varnish. Deepen the grain of the oak by rubbing firmly in the direction of the grain with a wire brush. Colour with red tinted liming wax (see steps 1–4, page 32). Cut new baise bases from the self-adhesive variety. From the long side of a sheet of thin cream card cut a 12 cm (4¾ in) strip. Use the rose bouquet template on page 104 to cut a stencil and use pinks, greens and a yellow paint to stencil the shade with a brush. Lightly mark 1 cm (⅜ in) measurements down both long sides on the front and back of the card. At every second mark on the front, place a steel rule across the card. Fold the card up against the edge of the rule to crease, using a blunt instrument – the handle of a teaspoon would be suitable. Repeat on the back, folding along alternate marks. Form creases along the entire length of the card to pleat it.

2 With right sides pushed together, make holes for the ribbon along the top edge, using a one-hole punch. Make the hole through two layers of a back-facing pleat. Repeat on every back-facing pleat, punching the hole at the same distance, about 3 mm (⅛ in) from the top edge each time.

3 Overlap the first and last pleats to form a circle, keeping the stencilling on the outside. Stick the overlap down with general purpose glue. Starting opposite the overlap, thread a 1 m (39 in) length of 6 mm (¼ in) wide ribbon through the punched holes. Work on the right side, threading the ribbon through both holes of a front-facing pleat each time. Form a narrow top edge to the shade by gathering the ribbon. Tie the ribbon ends in a bow and trim off any excess.The pleated shade should be placed on a special carrier, which fits over the top of the candle fitted in the base. Never leave a lit candle unattended or within reach of a child.

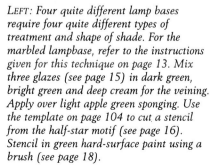

LEFT: *Four quite different lamp bases require four quite different types of treatment and shape of shade. For the marbled lampbase, refer to the instructions given for this technique on page 13. Mix three glazes (see page 15) in dark green, bright green and deep cream for the veining. Apply over light apple green sponging. Use the template on page 104 to cut a stencil from the half-star motif (see page 16). Stencil in green hard-surface paint using a brush (see page 18).*

CHINA BASE

1 To create a stone-like finish, like porphyry, paint a china lamp base surface with an ox-blood shade of oil-based paint. Allow to dry. Mix up glazes (see page 15) in yellow, black and gold and use in this order. Dip the end of a large stencil brush in each glaze in turn and spray onto the base by scratching the ends of the bristles with the tip of the forefinger to flick the paint on in spots.

2 Stencil the border motif in gold – it is subtle in feel like the porphyry. Gold stencil paint in a cream form is not too harsh – some golds are very bright. Match the stencil to the base – this classical shape needed a classical image. Cut a fleur-de-lys stencil from the template on page 104. Hold in place on a bought lampshade with fingers as well as spray adhesive and stencil in gold acrylic paint using a brush.

HANDMADE GIFTWRAP

A BEAUTIFULLY wrapped present is a delight to receive, but one wrapped in hand-printed paper is quite wonderful! It is not difficult to stencil and make a gift box, or to give a plain book a stunning cover. Opening a hand-made card, too, shows much time and thought went into the greeting. Stencil tissue paper for packing, coloured card for postcards, even humble brown parcel paper can be subtly enhanced with gold stencilling.

BOOK JACKET

1 Cut endpapers the size of the book cover and a piece of plain paper this size plus 2.5 cm (1 in). Using the templates on page 103 cut and paint the lily, thistle and daffodil motifs onto the endpapers and jacket. Centre the book over the wrong side of the paper and trim the corners, leaving 3 mm (⅛ in) of paper at the points. Make slits at the spine. Glue the wrong side of the jacket to the book. Close the book, sticking turnings to the inside. Glue on end papers. Trim excess paper off at the spine.

GIFTWRAP

1 Use dandelion leaves, ivy or flower head to achieve 'reverse' stencilling. Lay them at random on paper. Thin acrylic paint slightly with water, here gold and old copper were used, dip the end of a stencil brush in it and flick the bristles with a forefinger to produce a fine spray. Remove the leaves or flower heads. Alternatively, stencil coloured or textured paper with a repeating pattern. Use the templates on page 103 to cut fritillaria and holly stencils (see page 16) and stencil with a brush (see page 18) in green, purple and red hard-surface paints.

GIFT TAG

1 Use the offcuts from making the gift box to stencil gift and name tags. To trim off the excess card around the stencilling cut straight lines, using a steel rule and a sharp craft knife or scalpel, but stop cutting where the stencilling overlaps. Trim around these overlaps by hand to give an interesting outline. In one corner, use a hole punch to make a hole to thread the ribbon through.

ABOVE: Purchase thin coloured card, which comes in a wonderful array of colours, from good stationers and art stores to make cards, gift boxes and tags. Make book jackets from heavy, good quality paper – it needs to be strong, hard-wearing, but pliable. Stencil your card with any of the motifs illustrated here to produce a personal and individual accompaniment to your gifts.

GREETING CARDS

1 Cut window mount cards from thin coloured card to measure 33 x 15 cm (13 x 6 in). Fold in three, making folds as step 2 of the gift box. Cut a window from the centre section. Measure the width of your card aperture and add 1 cm (¼ in) to either side. Lay a steel rule on a piece of textured paper and gently tear the paper towards you to produce a feathered edge. Tear again at right angles to form small pieces that fit the card appertures.

2 Use the cherub and fritillaria templates on page 103 to stencil the torn paper in gold, green and purple stencil paints with the brush method. Glue the stencilled paper to the wrong side of the first section. Glue around the wrong side of the window and fold over the first section, sticking it in place. Add decorative flourishes with coloured marker pens. Mark lines lightly in pencil around the aperture of the card, then draw over them, using the marker pen against a bevelled ruler face down on the card to prevent ink running under.

GIFT BOX

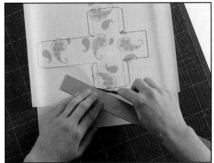

1 Draw off the template for a gift box on page 103 onto tracing paper. Use this as a guide to the size of area that needs stencilling. Referring to the paisley group template on page 103, cut a stencil and paint a repeating paisley pattern onto a piece of thin, coloured card. Use the brush method and green, yellow, mauve and maroon stencil or acrylic paints. To cut out the box, lay the tracing over the card, tape in place with masking tape and cut out carefully along the solid lines only, using a sharp craft knife or scalpel on a cutting board.

2 Using the tracing as a guide, score lightly along the dotted lines with the knife on the stencilled side of the card. Bend carefully at the score lines until a right angle is formed in each case. Spread general purpose glue on the four tabs of the 'cross bar' and glue to the plain side of the 'upright' bar, forming a box. Fold down the lid, tucking in the tab to close.

QUILL AND PEN STATIONERY SET

LETTER WRITING is still the most enduring form of communication, and all the more pleasurable if you have elegant accessories to use! Old letter racks, index files and blotters are easily found and can be renovated in subtle antique tones for the study, or in strong, eye-catching colours for the home office. Keep bills tidy, store family photographs and keep favourite magazine recipes in order with this attractive set of stationery items.

INDEX FILE

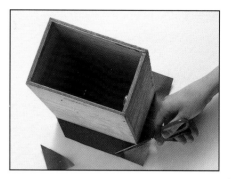

1 Remove the drawer from the box. Using a screwdriver with a fine head, carefully pull up the handle, this one was plastic, taking care not to damage the surface. Replace this with a brass handle or card carrier on completion.

2 This index file was made from a mixture of wood and thick cardboard. A wallpaper stripping agent will remove the paper from both if care is taken not to soak the cardboard too much. Once the liquid has soaked through the paper layer, gently prize it off with a metal scraper. Try to memorize the order of any overlaps or joins on the original paper.

3 Allow to dry thoroughly before covering with new paper. Select a good quality, plain one. Starting with the back of the box, cut the paper to fit, leaving 2 cm (¾ in) overlap all around. Paste the wrong side with PVA medium, press in place and trim the excess off the corners. Stick the overlapping paper to the sides. Cover the body of the box and the drawer in the same way and leave to dry. Use the templates on page102 to cut a quill and pen motif and two small oak leaf stencils (see page 16). Stencil with a brush (see page 18) in red, green, navy, black and gold hard-surface paints. Mask off the oak leaf design around the pen and quill when stencilling these to prevent colours from accidentally mixing.

LETTER RACK

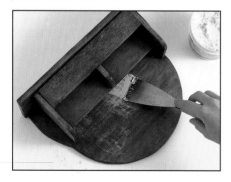

BLOTTER

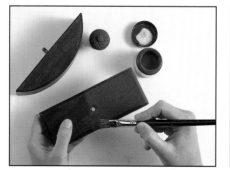

1 Remove the varnish finish from the wood (see page 12). It is at this point that the final finish must be decided on. Should the wood turn out to have beautiful graining it would be a shame to paint it. Fill any holes or scratches with fine surface filler, using a metal filler knife. Sand smooth when dry (see page 12).

2 The base feet and the original thirties plastic feet on this letter rack were replaced. Where possible, use the original screw holes, drilling holes to match in the new base piece. Tiny wooden door handles were used as replacement feet. Stick in place with wood glue. Apply two coats of eggshell in two shades of blue. In a well-ventilated room, clean the stencils cut for the index file with cellulose thinner. Stencil the motifs onto the letter rack as described for the index file.

1 Gilding is a wonderful method of creating instant age and makes a very ordinary object look expensive. Purchase red fontenay paste, gilt cream and optional gilt patina pencils from good art stores. Prepare the surface of an old blotter to reveal bare wood by stripping or sanding off old paint or varnish. Paint the handle and top of the blotter with fonteney paste. Allow to dry. Paint the curved underpart with two coats of blue eggshell. Leave to dry.

2 Paint over the red fontenay paste with gilt cream, using a stiffish brush. Dry, then sand off gently in places with fine grade wire wool to reveal the red layer beneath. With a clean cloth, buff to a soft sheen. The object can be left like this or more ageing and highlights added with patina pencils. Crayon them on in tiny lines or in small areas. Refer to step 3 of the index file to decorate the curved underpart of the blotter by stencilling with the small oak leaf motifs

CANDLESTICKS

1 The original finish on these candlesticks was so fine they only needed a light rub with medium grade wire wool to give a 'key' for the paint. Wrap the steel wool around an area and rotate the candlestick within it, to create a smooth surface. Finish with fine grade wool and paint with two coats of blue eggshell. The metal areas were painted in copper, an artist's brush being dipped into a small amount of paint sprayed into the lid of the can. Clean brushes in white spirit.

2 To unify the metal and wood and create an up-to-the-minute look, try a verdigris effect on the metal. Verdigris is traditionally done in shades of green but use blue tones here. Follow the verdigris directions on page 14 to make up two blue pastes. Take care not to get it on the paintwork and wipe off immediately with a damp cloth if you do. Sand carefully with fine wire wool to reveal the copper paint. Position the small oak leaf stencils cut for the index file on areas large enough for decoration. Stencil as before.

ABOVE : Adapt a space under the stairs or display stationery items in a corner to show them to their best advantage. They will look particularly attractive arranged on natural wood in dark, rich colours. The candlesticks can also be used as table centrepieces or to decorate a mantlepiece.

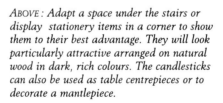

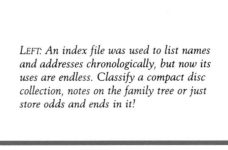

LEFT: An index file was used to list names and addresses chronologically, but now its uses are endless. Classify a compact disc collection, notes on the family tree or just store odds and ends in it!

PICTURES AND
FRAMES

IF EVERY PICTURE tells a story, then its stencilled frame tells another one! Old pictures and frames are so often designated to the scrap heap, but take a second look at them, they can become individual works of art with a little imagination. The easiest frames to stencil are wide and flat or with a gentle curve. But stencilling does not have to be confined to the frame – a large mount is ideal – or try stencilling the picture.

RIGHT: Old frames can be given a new lease of life with decorative stencilling while smaller pictures can be given additional impact by echoing the motif on the mount.

FRUIT FRAME

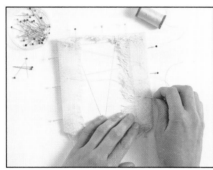

1 Mount a piece of embroidery with a fruit motif by cutting a piece of white card to the outside measurements of the embroidered area, allowing a border all around. Place the card on the wrong side of the work and fold the excess fabric over the card. Secure by pushing pins into the edge of the card all around. Using a needle and buttonhole thread, secure the embroidery with stitches from top to bottom and from side to side. Oversew to secure and remove the pins. Ask a picture framing service to cut a mount to the measurements of your frame and with a circular aperture. Use the template on page 105 to cut a cherry stencil. With a brush and using gold hard-surface paint, stencil the cherries and three leaves only onto the corners of the mount, masking off the part of the stencil not needed. In red, orange, green and gold paints, stencil the whole motif onto the corners of the frame.

LEFT: A large mount is very dramatic and leads the eye into the picture. Echo the subject matter subtly in gold stencilling and emphasize the frame edge, rubbing on acrylic gold paint with the tip of your finger.

SILHOUETTES FRAME

1 For the mount, measure the recess of the frame and cut dark blue artist's card to this size using a sharp scalpel, a steel rule

and a cutting board. On the wrong side mark two 4 x 5 cm (1½ x 2 in) apertures 1.5 cm (½ in) apart for the silhouettes with a fine marker pen. Cut these openings, finishing the cuts exactly on the marked lines. Cut a piece of white card to the same size as the mount. Lay the mount over the right side of the white card and lightly mark the openings in pencil. Use the templates on page 105 to cut and stencil two silhouettes onto the white card using black paint and a stencil brush (see pages 16 and 18). To verdigris a metal frame, follow the instructions given on pages 14–15. Replace the mount in the frame, followed by the stencilled silhouettes and backing board.

Floral Frame

1 Take the backing board off the frame and prepare the wooden surface as described on page 12, including the final sanding. It is possible to lighten wood a little with a proprietary wood bleach. Wear rubber gloves and use a glass bowl. Dip a paintbrush in the liquid and paint on sparingly. Leave to dry and re-apply if necessary. Wash off and allow to dry. Cut three stencils from the rose and rosebud templates on page 105. Stencil the motifs onto the frame with a brush (see page 18), using two shades of green, and red, pink and white hard-surface paint. Cut a cardboard mount as for the silhouette frame, making a 5 cm (2 in) square aperture in the centre. Place the mount on large-checked blue fabric, cut 2.5 cm (1 in) larger all around. Trim away the fabric at each corner. Apply general purpose glue to the turnings and press to the wrong side of mount, keeping the fabric taut on the front. Snip into the corners of the central opening and glue the turnings to the mount in the same way.

2 Use the template on page 105 to cut a floral bouquet stencil. Stencil using the brush method in red, yellow and green paints onto the centre of a piece of white card. Cut to the same size as the mount. Fit the fabric mount then the stencilled picture into the frame. Replace the backing board. Moisten the gummed side of 5 cm (2 in) tape with a damp sponge and glue onto the back where the backing board and frame meet. Push the backing board down firmly. Screw in screw eyes with rings on either side of the frame and attach picture wire.

Mirror

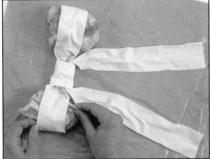

1 Remove the glass from a circular mirror frame approximately 30 cm (12 in) in diameter. Paint using acrylic paint in a copper tone. Replace the mirror. On white cartridge paper and using the oak leaf templates on page 105 to cut stencils, stencil 18 leaves with a stencil brush and acrylic paints in metallic shades of gold, bronze, red and copper. Using small, sharp scissors, cut around each leaf. Use diluted PVA medium to stick in place, overlapping one another and breaking onto the mirror surface. Clean off any glue with a damp cloth.

2 From a 10 cm (4 in) wide strip of cotton fabric cut two pieces 35 cm (14 in) long for tails, one 60 cm (23½ in) length for loops and one 18 cm (7 in) length for a tie. Lay on a surface that can be cleaned. Paint each one on the wrong side with PVA adhesive and fold in the side edges to meet in the centre. Open out a carrier bag and on it place the ends of the loop together. Nip the centre of the circle with the 'tie' and insert the 'tails' under the tie. Support the loops with screwed up plastic bags and leave to dry. Paint with bronze acrylic paint.

Goose Frame

1 This charming embroidery was very badly marked as water, coloured by the wood mount, had stained the fabric. Remove the worst areas of discolouration and any spots with well-diluted household bleach applied on a cotton wool wrapped stick (try a test area first). Lay the embroidery on kitchen paper towel and gently rub with the wet stick. Replace the sticks frequently.

2 Before remounting the embroidery, soak it in a solution of biological washing powder. Lay on kitchen paper towel to dry. Press. Cut a piece of mounting board with an adhesive surface, available from craft stores, on one side to fit the embroidery. Peel off the paper covering and carefully lay the wrong side of the embroidery over the sticky area, starting from one corner and smoothing out any creases. The oak-veneered mount on this picture was badly warped by water. If you have a similar problem, lay the mount on plenty of damp kitchen paper and cover with the same. Cover the entire area of the mount with a large book or similar and pile on a few more to produce a good weight. Leave for several days to dry.

ABOVE: Pick out details like flat edges in matching paint. The colour scheme is obviously red and blue. Both are present in the braid, which not only adds a finishing, decorative touch but unites the two colours.

FARMHOUSE KITCHENWARE

OLD FASHIONED enamelware is making a comeback in the kitchen. Copies of 1950s designs can be bought again, while original pieces can be found at flea markets and second-hand stores. These are often dented or chipped and are not to be recommended for use in the preparation of food. However, they are wonderful stencilled as decorative pieces out on display. Match them up with other items to give total co-ordination.

SCALES

1 The weighing bowl on this basic set of scales was made from tin. Much better looking are brass or copper bowls. Cheat a little and colour the bowl with brass, copper or bronze spray paint in a can. This bowl was painted brass to match the lovely brass weights that were bought with it. Two iron weights that were also part of the set were given several coats of blackboard paint before being stencilled to match the scales.

HERB DRAWERS

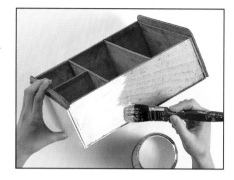

1 Create a set of herb drawers from an old miniature chest. This one, though crudely made from cheap timber, had good proportions and lovely china handles. These were carefully unscrewed and the old paint cleaned off with fine wire wool and paint stripper. Use rubber gloves if you can, or coat your hands with barrier cream to protect them. Strip off the old finish and sand smooth (see page 12). The entire surface need not be painted as a little natural wood showing adds to the country feel. Cover the areas to be painted with acrylic primer, masking the edges if necessary. Acrylic primer dries quickly, making handling easier when the whole object is not being painted. Cover the primed areas with pale green eggshell paint. Allow to dry. Remove masking tape.

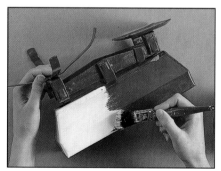

2 Paint the base of the scales with red oxide metal primer (an awkward shape like these scales may need two coats to cover all the nooks and crannies). Then coat in a rich cream oil-based paint such as eggshell. Painting such a pale colour over the dark metal primer will require several coats. Dry well between coats.

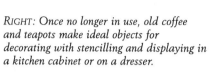
RIGHT: Once no longer in use, old coffee and teapots make ideal objects for decorating with stencilling and displaying in a kitchen cabinet or on a dresser.

RIGHT: Old kitchenware often has particularly appealing shapes. You will probably have some old kitchenware yourself in your attic or storeroom

BELOW: Pick items with varying shapes and heights to make an interesting display of kitchenware. These charming pieces, gathered from a variety of sources, are painted in clotted cream and herb shades and decorated with appropriate country images to fit the style and atmosphere of the kitchen decorated in farmhouse style.

TEAPOT AND COFFEEPOT

1 Even badly stained enamel, as often found in old teapots, can be cleaned effectively. Soak in a bowl of cold water and biological washing powder. Leave for a couple of days if necessary and scrub intermittantly with a pan scourer which will not scratch the surface.

2 Fill any chips or dents with two-part car filler, available from car accessory stores, following the manufacturer's directions for use. Any rust should be treated with a rust removal product. Paint the object inside and out with red oxide metal primer. In damp weather, the inside may take several days to dry. Paint on several coats of green or cream eggshell paint. Allow each coat to dry thoroughly before painting the next.

STENCILLING

1 Use the templates on page 107 to cut stencils of the floral and cow motifs (see page 16). Stencil onto the tea and coffee pot base and lid, the base of the scales and iron weights and onto the front of each herb drawer. Stencil with a brush (see page 18) in soft shades of green, pink, blue and brown hard-surface paints. Use spray adhesive and masking tape to keep the stencils in place. Pick out any details on the pots using one of the stencilling colours and an artist's paint brush to colour knobs and rims. To age your kitchenware, try crackling it, using one of the varieties of crackling varnish available from good paint and art stores. Follow the manufacturer's directions carefully.

2 When the crackling is quite dry, make up an ageing solution to patinate or darken the cracks. Mix some artist's oil paint in a burnt umber shade with a little white spirit to the consistency of double or heavy cream. Paint it all over – do not worry if it looks like a dreadful mistake. Allow to dry for a few minutes before wiping off the excess with a clean rag. Leave the paint in the cracks to dry. The entire surface of your kitchenware will be slightly darkend by using this treatment.

Diagrams and Stencils

The following pages present the templates for the stencils used in this book. To reproduce the templates at the same size as originally used for each project, either trace the motif straight from the page where the motif is designated 'same size', or enlarge the motif to the percentage given on a photocopier. Otherwise, use a photocopier to enlarge or reduce the motif to the size required for your model.

A number of motifs will require you to cut two or more separate stencils where one colour is stencilled over another (see pages 16–17). The number of stencils to be cut is specified in each case.

ROSE CHEST OF DRAWERS
page 24

BOW
Enlarge by 150%
Cut 1

SMALL ROSE
Same size
Cut 1

LARGE ROSE
Enlarge by 150%
Cut 1

ORIENTAL WARDROBE
page 26

DRAGONFLY 1
Enlarge by 200%
Cut 1

DRAGONFLY 2
Enlarge by 200%
Cut 1

Place to fold

CHINESE CIRCLE
Enlarge by 200%
Cut 1

TREE SECTION (LEFT)
Enlarge by 200%
Cut 1

BIRD
Enlarge by 200%
Cut 1

87

FLORAL CIRCULAR TABLE
page 28

OUTER MOTIF
Enlarge by 150%
Cut 3

CENTRAL MOTIF
Enlarge by 150%
Cut 1

TARTAN DINING CHAIRS
page 30

TARTAN
Enlarge by 200%
Cut 3

HEART CUPBOARD
page 32

HEART & RIBBON
Same size
Cut 1

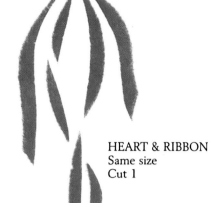

GRID
Enlarge by 150%
Cut 1

ART NOUVEAU FIREPLACE
page 34

MOTIF
Enlarge by 150%
Cut 1

FLOWER
Enlarge by 150%
Cut 1

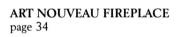

SEASIDE LINEN BASKET
page 36

SHELL
Enlarge by 200%
Cut 1

SHELL
Enlarge by 200%
Cut 1

STARFISH
Enlarge by 200%
Cut 1

NOAH'S ARK COT QUILT
page 40

LION
Enlarge by 150%
Cut 3

ARK
Enlarge by 150%
Cut 1

ELEPHANTS
Enlarge by 150%
Cut 1

SQUIRREL
Enlarge by150%
Cut 2

NOAH
Enlarge by150%
Cut 2

NOAH'S WIFE
Enlarge by 150%
Cut 2

GIRAFFE
Enlarge by 150%
Cut 2

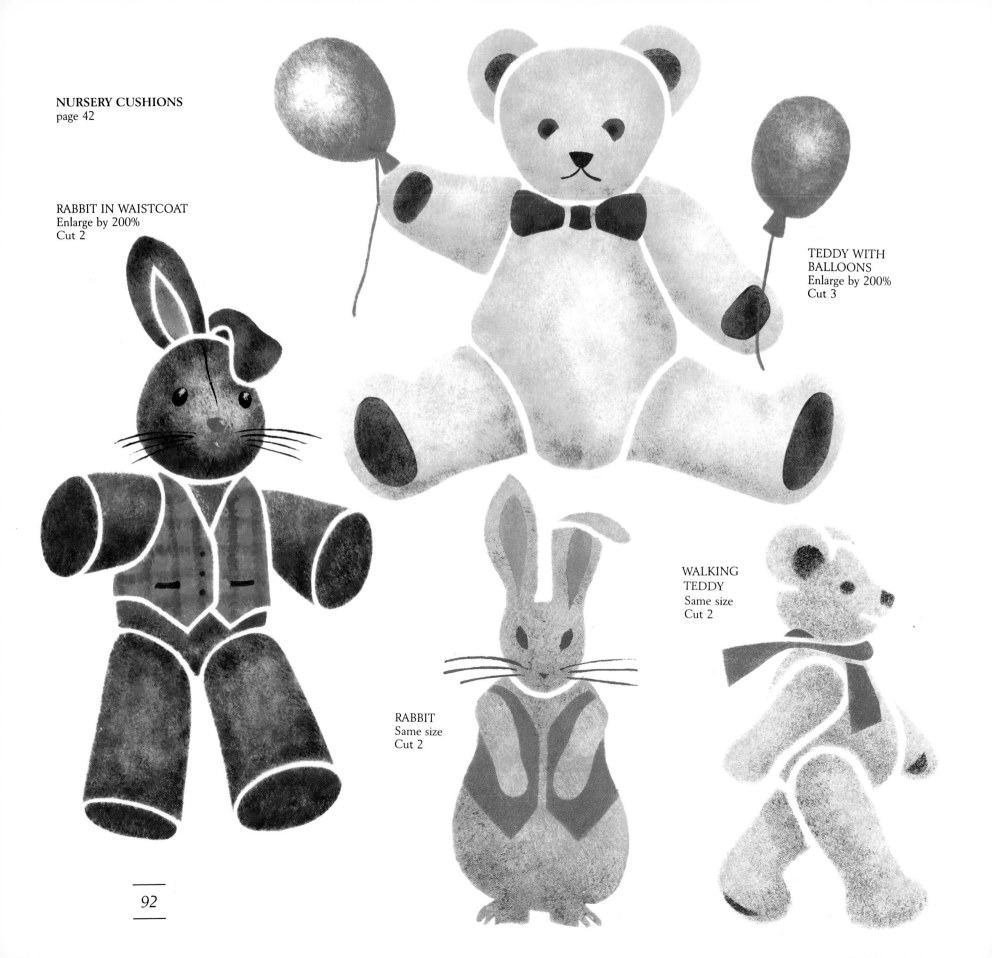

NURSERY CUSHIONS
page 42

RABBIT IN WAISTCOAT
Enlarge by 200%
Cut 2

TEDDY WITH
BALLOONS
Enlarge by 200%
Cut 3

WALKING
TEDDY
Same size
Cut 2

RABBIT
Same size
Cut 2

EGYPTIAN BATHROOM
page 44

FLOWER
Same size
Cut 1

PALM TREE
Same size
Cut 1

FLOWER
Same size
Cut 1

WATER CARRIER
Same size
Cut 1

SPHINX
Same size
Cut 1

CLASSIC RUG
page 46

CLASSIC MOTIF 1
Same size
Cut 1

CLASSIC MOTIF 2
Same size
Cut 1

SEA CREATURES DECKCHAIR
page 48

SEA MONSTER
Enlarge by 150%
Cut 1

FISH
Same size
Cut 1

SEA MONSTER
Same size
Cut 1

95

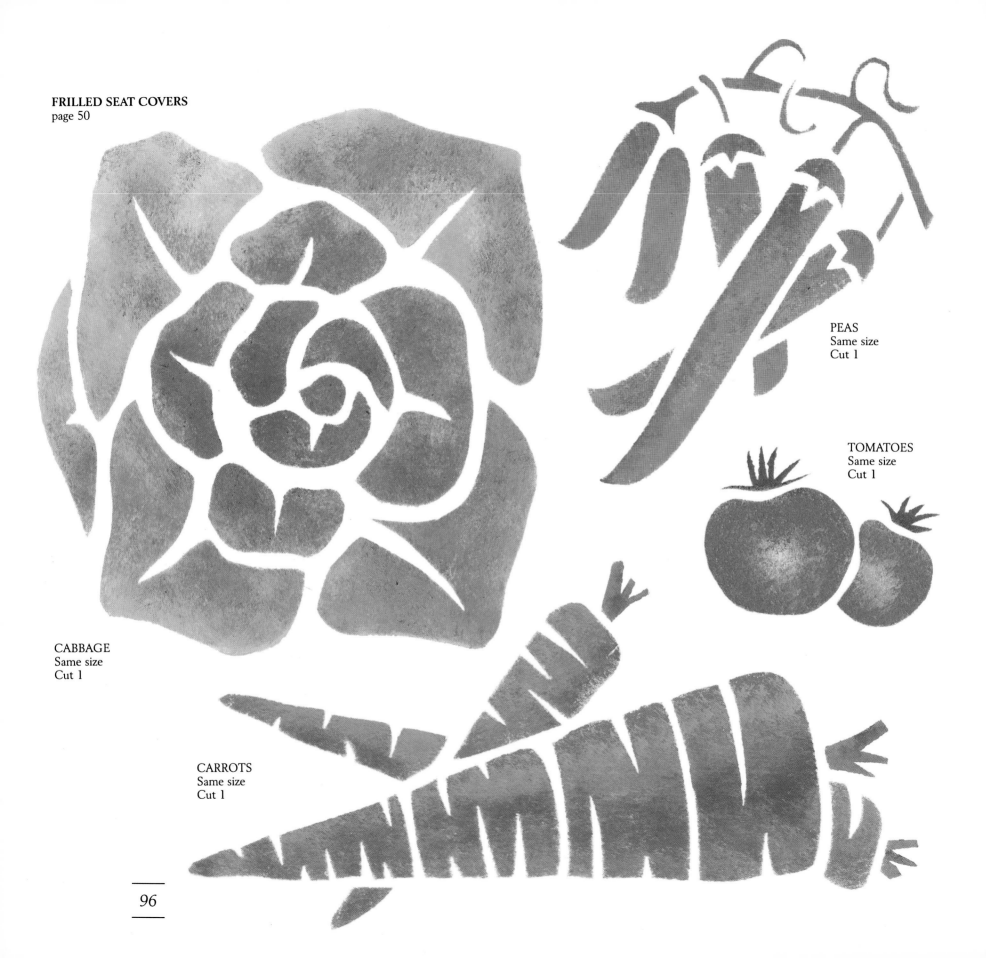

FRILLED SEAT COVERS
page 50

PEAS
Same size
Cut 1

TOMATOES
Same size
Cut 1

CABBAGE
Same size
Cut 1

CARROTS
Same size
Cut 1

96

FLORAL CUPBOARD
page 52

ROSEBUD
Same size
Cut 1

ROSE
Enlarge by 200%
Cut 1

TILED WALL
page 56

TILE
Enlarge by 150%
Cut 1

GEOMETRIC PATIO & POTS
page 58

POT BORDER 1
Enlarge by 150%
Cut 1

POT STAR
Enlarge by 150%
Cut 1

POT BORDER 2
Enlarge by 150%
Cut 1

MOSAIC BORDER
Enlarge by 150%
Cut 1

MOSAIC CORNER
Enlarge by 150%
Cut 1

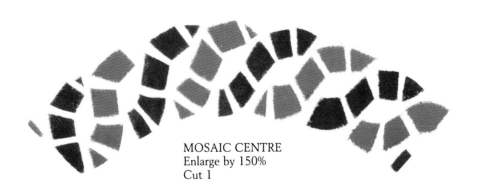

MOSAIC CENTRE
Enlarge by 150%
Cut 1

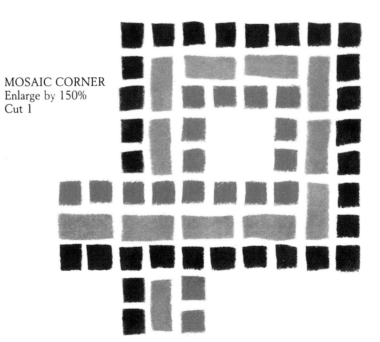

FRENCH BREAD BIN
page 60

TREES, HEDGE, GATE
Enlarge by 150%
Cut 1

CHIVES
Enlarge by 150%
Cut 2

MOUSE
Same size
Cut 2

CAT
Enlarge by 200%
Cut 2

CHILD'S DRESSER
page 62

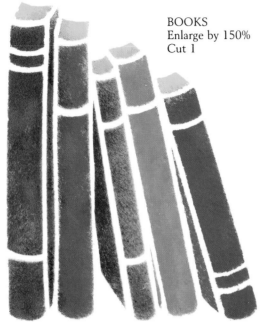

BOOKS
Enlarge by 150%
Cut 1

STANDING DOLL
Enlarge by 150%
Cut 2

SITTING DOLL
Enlarge by 150%
Cut 2

PLATE
Enlarge by 150%
Cut 1

CUP AND SAUCER
Enlarge by 150%
Cut 1

TEDDY
Enlarge by 150%
Cut 1

GARDEN SCREEN
page 64

HANGING BASKET
Enlarge by 200%
Cut 1

HERB POT
Enlarge by 200%
Cut 1

BUTTERFLY
Enlarge by 200%
Cut 1

TRELLIS
Enlarge by 300%
Cut 1

CONTAINER
Enlarge by 300%
Cut 1

HERB POT
Enlarge by 200%
Cut 1

101

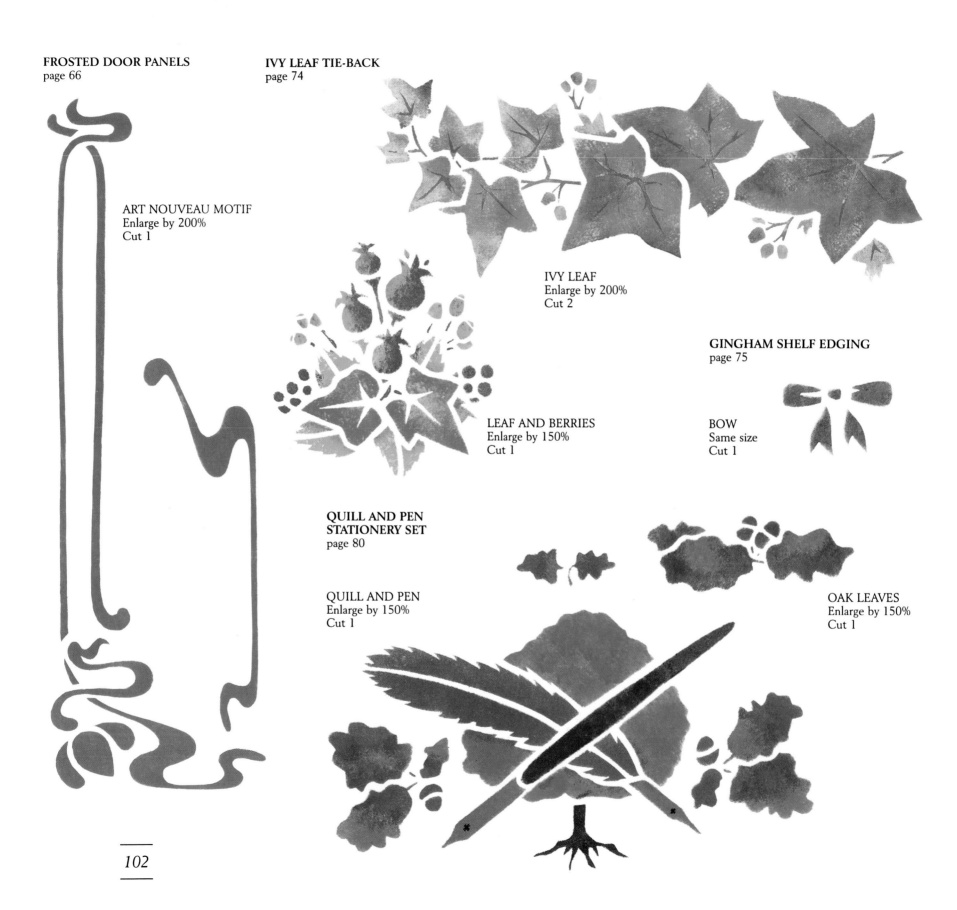

FROSTED DOOR PANELS
page 66

IVY LEAF TIE-BACK
page 74

ART NOUVEAU MOTIF
Enlarge by 200%
Cut 1

IVY LEAF
Enlarge by 200%
Cut 2

GINGHAM SHELF EDGING
page 75

LEAF AND BERRIES
Enlarge by 150%
Cut 1

BOW
Same size
Cut 1

**QUILL AND PEN
STATIONERY SET**
page 80

QUILL AND PEN
Enlarge by 150%
Cut 1

OAK LEAVES
Enlarge by 150%
Cut 1

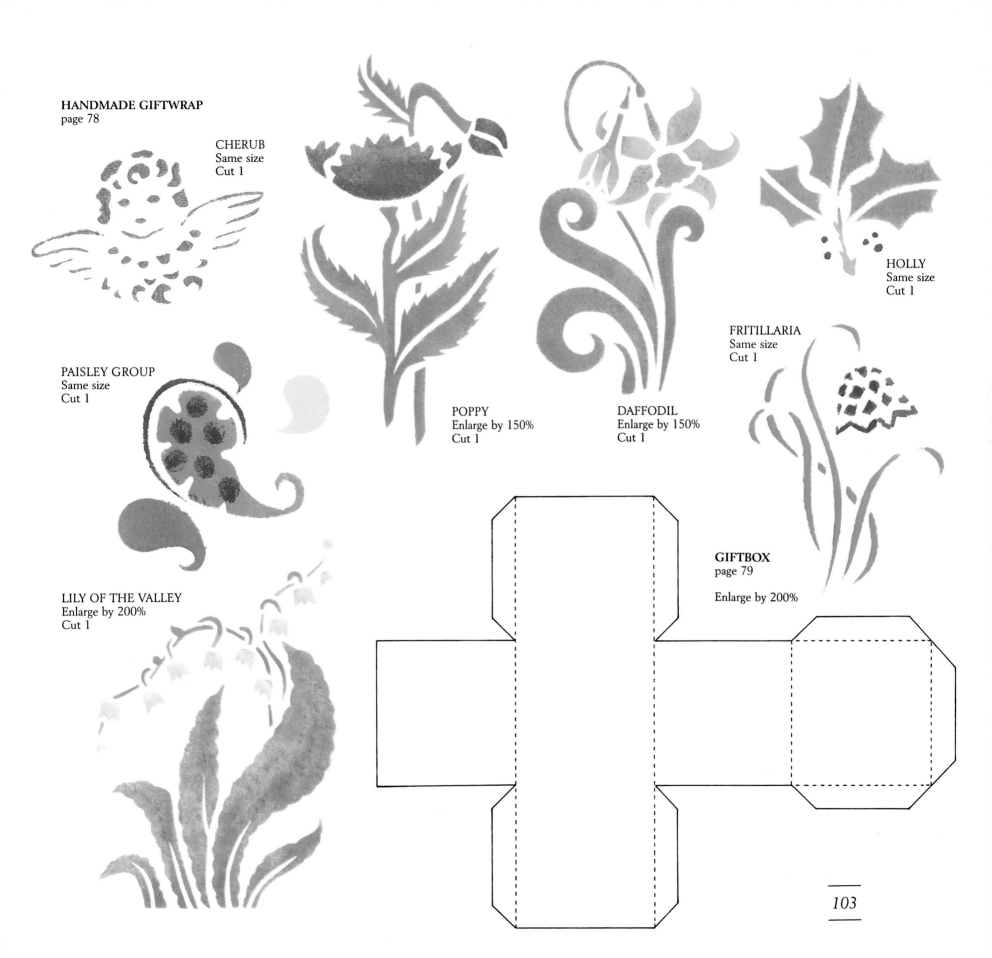

HANDMADE GIFTWRAP
page 78

CHERUB
Same size
Cut 1

HOLLY
Same size
Cut 1

FRITILLARIA
Same size
Cut 1

PAISLEY GROUP
Same size
Cut 1

POPPY
Enlarge by 150%
Cut 1

DAFFODIL
Enlarge by 150%
Cut 1

GIFTBOX
page 79

Enlarge by 200%

LILY OF THE VALLEY
Enlarge by 200%
Cut 1

103

DECORATIVE LIGHTING
page 76

BORDER LEAVES
Same size
Cut 1

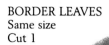

SMALL LEAF
Same size
Cut 1

CLASSICAL BORDER
Same size
Cut 1

FLEUR-DE-LYS
Same size
Cut 1

ROSE BOUQUET
Same size
Cut 1

HALF STAR
Same size
Cut 1

PICTURES AND FRAMES
page 82

SILHOUETTE 1
Same size
Cut 1

SILHOUETTE 2
Same size
Cut 1

FLORAL BOUQUET
Same size
Cut 1

ROSE
Same size
Cut 1

ROSEBUDS
Same size
Cut 1 each

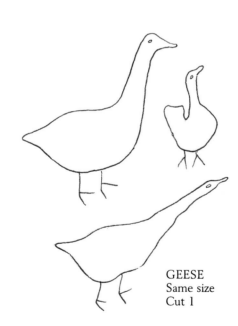

GEESE
Same size
Cut 1

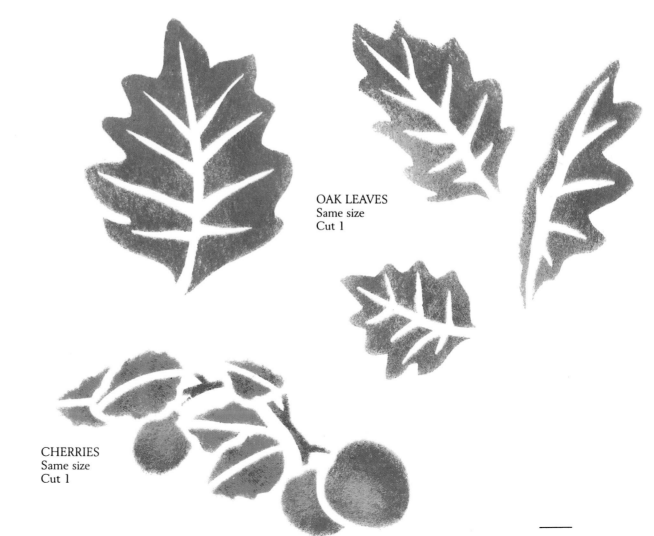

OAK LEAVES
Same size
Cut 1

CHERRIES
Same size
Cut 1

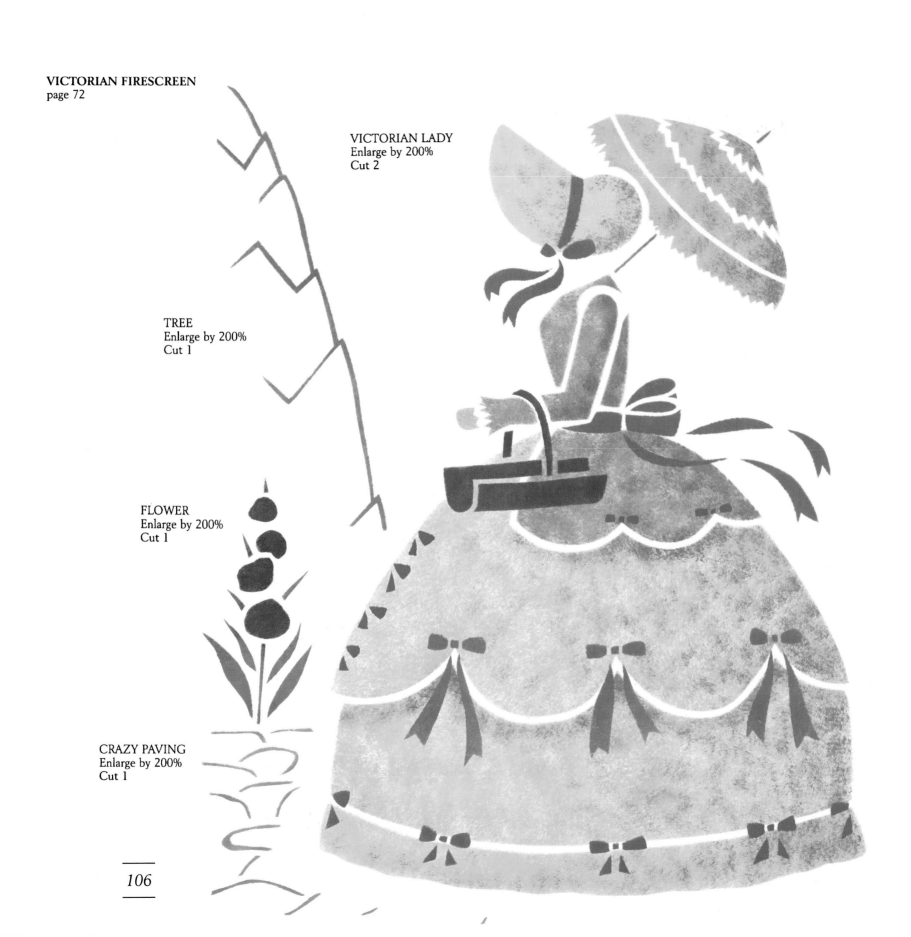

VICTORIAN FIRESCREEN
page 72

VICTORIAN LADY
Enlarge by 200%
Cut 2

TREE
Enlarge by 200%
Cut 1

FLOWER
Enlarge by 200%
Cut 1

CRAZY PAVING
Enlarge by 200%
Cut 1

FARMHOUSE KITCHENWARE
page 84

FLORAL MOTIFS
Same size
Cut 1 of each

COW
Same size
Cut 1

Acknowledgements

The author is grateful to the following for supplying materials and services for this book:

For decorating materials: C. Brewer & Sons Ltd, Portsmouth Road, Surbiton, Surrey, KT6 5QB; for carpets: Curragh-Tintawn Ltd, Claire House, Bridge Street, Leatherhead, Surrey, KT22 8BZ; for the gothic screen (pages 64–65): Dormy House, Sterling Park, East Portway Industrial Estate, Andover, Hants, SP10 3TZ; for Colorfun Soft Fabric Paints: Dylon International Ltd, Worsley Bridge Road, Lower Sydenham, London, SE26 5HD; for aerosol paints (pages 48–49): Hammerite Products Ltd, Prudhoe, Northumberland, NE42 6LP; for furniture wax and other materials: Liberon Waxes Ltd, Mountfield Industrial Estate, Learoyd Road, New Romney, Kent, TN28 8XU; for the roller blind (pages 44–45): Luxaflex Blinds, Hunter Douglas Ltd, The Industrial Estate, Larkhall, Lanarkshire, ML9 2PD: for ceramic varnish (pages 44–45): Pavilion Originals Ltd, 6a Howe Street, Edinburgh, EH3 6TD; for decorative paint finishes: Polyvine Ltd, Vine House, Rockhampton, Berkeley, Gloucestershire, GL13 9DT; for wallpapers: Arthur Sanderson & Sons Ltd, 112–120 Brompton Road, London, SW3 1JJ; for stripping the large items: John Scales at Southside Strippers, 19 Summerstown, Tooting, London, SW17 0BQ.